Chapter 23

J Nicoel Western

1

My life was a mess. Not a catastrophic, messy mess. More like a what-happens-next type of mess. It's all my fault I suppose. Not that I'd be eager to point fingers at anyone else besides myself, but because I've always been completely aware of my choice to live life day by day, somewhat fifty percent oblivious and one hundred percent open minded. Oh, and I'm also not much of a finger pointer.

"You're so nice!" "You're so fun!" "You're so loud!" I've always been told. If only everyone knew just how mean, boring, and quiet I knew I could be. My all-time favorite, though? *"You're so real!"* And while I've always just replied with my overly awkward smile, isn't that how we should all be? "Real?" I mean, come on. The only other option is fake. And we all somewhat have complete control over ourselves. Wouldn't real be the most obvious personality trait to choose?

...

I'm a child of God. I'd like to say I'm just like any other Christian, but I believe I'm not.

Honestly, growing up in a Baptist church I was always confused with whether to call myself a Baptist or a Christian. I still don't know the difference. There are too many differences in religion. Who's to say who's right? Not me. Now while I've made some pretty "non-Christian" like choices over the years, I've always been very aware of my relationship with God. I was the girl turning down the music drunk on the way to the club to pray over myself and my friends.

    That's the amazing thing about God. He sees and knows our sins, yet loves us just the same. I believe we are all children of God, no matter how we perceive Him, we are His children. And as His children I believe we are to live the best that we can. No matter the choices we make, no matter the sins we constantly commit, He loves us, and as long as we stay close with Him and as long as we know and choose to be good people, then we are doing His work. And no matter the struggles that come along in life, we have nothing to worry about because our time here is only temporary, but our time with Him will be eternal.

I believe He uses each of us to speak and be His voice. I believe this more than anything. I believe He is constantly using me to do His work as well as putting people in my life to be His voice and His reminder to me that He's here.

...

Well, before long I was twenty-three. Twenty-three and beginning a new chapter. That's one thing about me – I've always used ages to base my life. First drink at fifteen, first love at sixteen, the terrible twos (twenty-two, the only year I've ever been "in trouble." Don't drink and drive. Not even one long island ice tea at the beginning of the night). I once tried to convince an ex to wait until I was twenty-three and had experienced life on my own and I'd give forever with him a shot. He didn't like that idea. Fast forward. Twenty-three.

JJ, the craziest love I've ever had, had been in prison for a little over half a year. And quite frankly that's the only thing that could keep the two of us apart. Not the physical abuse, not the lying, not the cheating, not the mental abuse, or even our parents pleading for each of us to let go. Only prison. And I'm still not pointing fingers. My fingers were too occupied writing him every day on my lunch break. (Insert rolling eyes emoji here.) That's an entire other mess. A catastrophic one.

It was time for me to get my life going. My life had always been going. But there for a while, my life felt as if it wasn't going much of anywhere at all. I was stuck not knowing who or what made me happy. Surely it was JJ, right? But now it was time for me to get going. Without JJ. Just me.

I had been working my dream job as a preschool teacher in the next town for a bit over a year, but being a money hungry, newly single, female in her early twenties who had yet to have kids, I wanted more. I quit going to college not long after I met JJ and started spending all of my time with him and failing out of school. I figured I had better get a second job. I only worked with women and was paid didley squat and was only receiving a check every other week. I was a natural at serving, so surely my homeboy Travis from high school could hook me up with a gig at his father's restaurant, Savannah's. I was craving that constant cash flow received from tips.

I wanted to get an apartment. Living with my mom was great and affordable, but I was way past eager to completely change almost everything about my life on my new personal journey back into the world. The landlord at the apartments said she could get me in immediately.

How weird is it that the apartment I was put in was not only the apartment that was where I had my first drink at my friend's uncle's house when I was fifteen, but it was also my high school bestie's apartment when she got her first spot. I had literally partied in my new home for years before Madalynn and I moved in. Wild. That's how my life has always worked. The most ridiculous coincidences.

Madalynn is my ride or die. She knows all of my secrets, has seen most of what I've seen, has the most jacked up teeth and nappy blonde hair, hates fireworks, and loves rib bones. I picked her out before her eyes were open and have had her ever since. She was three when I was twenty-three. Still a pup I suppose, and as loyal as ever. I'd do experiments of opening up a box of pizza and putting it on the floor and she knew better than to eat it! She's never been on a leash and went where I went. We were both ready for this new chapter. And it was all happening so quickly.

Thanks to Travis and Rice, I got all moved in and was set. I had all the furniture I needed and they did almost all of the work for me. I've always been blessed with some pretty amazing friends. I was so ready for what was to come. Nothing felt better than having my own place. I was anxious for this chapter. Of course I wrote JJ to tell him about it. I was going to get another job, I got my own place, and I was making it. He said he was happy for me. So naturally, I believed him.

Travis got me on at Savannah's. I went in, talked about life that had nothing to do with work, told him when I could make it from job one to job two, and picked up my uniform.

Travis was going to be my boss. I mean, I felt like he was anyways. I suppose his father, Vince, was my boss.

Travis ran things for his father. Alex was his main man at the restaurant. I grew up with Alex. And by grew up I mean we went to the same junior and high school. He was much hotter now, like fifty pounds less hotter. Lol. But just a homeboy. My Russian homeboy. My boss at the preschool was cool with my schedule. I was set to go. Two jobs. New apartment. No more hustling. New chapter.

2

It was my first night at Savannah's. I got off work at the preschool, sped home to replace my red, awkward, somewhat tight-fitting polo with my new, overly sized, awkward-fitting black polo. I touched up my makeup, which consisted of applying another coat of mascara on top of the mascara I applied at seven that morning, put Madalynn in the bathroom after her walk, and headed out for my first night.

I'll never forget the first thing Vince said to me when I showed up.

"What kind of serving schedule starts at 5:45, 6 o'clock?"

Although his face was kind, his persona was always one of a mean guy. He was very monotone unless he was yelling or cursing at his sons. He was always nice to me. Always quick to give me a hard time. Always wearing a smirk that left one unable to distinguish whether he was happy or upset.

Travis showed me around in the back. I was anticipating working with such a chill cook staff. Travis's younger brother and crazy Eddie ran things in the back. I knew it was always going to be a good time. And I was right. I followed Travis through the metal swinging door that separated the front lobby from the kitchen and to the back where he was immediately called to help out on the line.

"You got this?" he asked.

"Yeah, sure," I could feel my eyes widen.

"Okay, good. Rosita will be training you." He walked off, grabbed a ticket, put it between his teeth, and quickly tied his apron.

I followed Rosita around and quickly realized it was going to be a piece of pie. I say piece of pie because Travis baked and sold the most delicious and beautiful pies. I had served at a few other restaurants in the past and this one seemed way more laid back than any before.

Savannah's had two wait staff areas, or wait stations, and we were stationed back in what we called the hidden one. The bus tub was full. The night was still early and somewhat dead. I had only been on for about thirty minutes. I grabbed the tub and told Rosita I'd take it to the back.

I rounded the wall of the main wait station and ran smack dab into a tall dark haired boy. The glasses in the bus tub clanked loudly and everyone in the lobby looked up at me for a second of silence before returning back to their conversations and dinner.

    Our eyes immediately met, of course. He was the same height as me. Something most six foot girls aren't used to. He dropped his phone on the shelf and grabbed onto the bus tub. I didn't let go. His crooked facial expression crept to the biggest smile. He pulled the tub out of my hands. The glasses clanked loudly again. Luckily not loud enough to re-interrupt everyone's dinner.

    Instead of taking the tub to the back, he set it on the shelf on top of his phone as well as some unused napkins. He stuck his hand out for me to shake. I looked at his hand, then back at him. I grabbed his hand and shook it.

    "I'm Jon," he said while still holding on to my hand, "and you're probably the most beautiful girl I've ever seen."

    "Oh." I said, feeling warmth in my cheeks, "I'm Jasmine. Travis's friend."

    Alex came through the swinging door. Jon picked up the tub and disappeared to the back and I went to find Rosita.

The rest of the night was a blur. It didn't take long for me to realize it was going to be easy work. Rosita, the other girls, Jon, and Alex were hard working so, I never felt like I needed to pick up anyone else's slack. We stayed busy. The food was amazing. The side work was a breeze and mopping was fun. The floor became so slippery as if you were gliding on ice. Mopping felt like you were risking your life. I had worked at five restaurants prior, but it was clear this was by far my favorite. Rosita was incredibly kind. My good friend Tabitha was going to start soon. Momma D was hilarious. Travis and the guys in the back were fun and constantly cracking jokes.

Jon only smiled at me the rest of the night. I found myself always smiling back in return. I didn't see him when I was on my way out. I rushed out to my car and was home by nine-thirty. I took Madalynn on a walk. I was asleep before ten-thirty. I crashed hard. This new chapter was going to be an exhausting one.

Before I knew it, it was eight in the morning and I was clocking on in my red polo. My day went as normal. My break started. I wrote JJ to tell him about my first night at the restaurant. And then it hit me: I had thought about Jon when I woke up that morning.

I tried pushing him out of my mind for the rest of the day. I found myself thinking of him again later on on my way out of my apartment door in my black polo as I walked back to my mirror to double check my appearance.

Lord, Jasmine. Get to work.

I clocked on and it was like I wasn't even trying to hide that I was looking around for Jon. No one knew though. Rosita came in and said I was following her for the night. Alex came in after her with Travis. Travis told me it was my last night training. He told me that if I could survive a Friday night training then I would be good to go.

No Jon. That was probably a good thing because no telling what school girl crush behavior I would have ridiculously trotted around with. This was definitely a new feeling for me. But even more definitely a weird one. I remember telling myself I was such a loser getting in my feels over being called beautiful. Surely he talks like that to everyone.

I have more of that mediocre kind of beauty. Pretty, but not hot. Cute, but not sexy.

He said beautiful, though. And that smile. And his height. And his hair.
Stop it, Jasmine.

3

The next night was rough. It was also my first night alone on the floor. No Rosita. However, that night I was stationed in the hidden section in the back with Jon.

"Why are you late?" He asked when I was putting my phone behind the sugar packets.

"I'm not," I replied without looking at him. "I just came from my other job and Travis worked with my schedule."

"You Travis's girl?"

"Homegirl," I replied, still without looking at him. I went to take my first table.

We were so busy that night, but Jon was a lot of help. He didn't let me empty the bus tub once. I felt like he was taking care of me. *Is this just him or does he like me?* I wondered.

Stop it, Jasmine.

The night finally came to an end. Jon vacuumed my section for me. I insisted I could do it.

"I'm sure you've got someone to rush home to." He smirked when he took the vacuum from me.

"Yeah, I do. Thanks."

I looked back as I walked away. He had his hand on his hip. Was he pretending to be on his phone? Then I heard a click. He was taking a picture!

My mouth fell open. I turned around to head to the back and busted my ass on Alex's freshly mopped floor. I turned back to look at Jon and he had disappeared. *What the? Where the hell did he go? Oh well.* I got up and went to the kitchen and conned Travis's brother into sharing his chicken strips with me while I did my back side work.

When Jon came into the back I did everything I could not to make eye contact with him.

I finished up. He finished up right as I did. I clocked out. He clocked out right as I did. I started walking out. He walked out right as I did.

What the hell? This black Mustang was not parked next to my car when I got to work.

"This your car?" I asked him.

He was only a foot or two behind me.

"Yep. My baby. What are you doing tonight? You in a rush?"

"I mean, I guess I've got to let Madalynn out."

"Madalynn?"

"Yep, Madalynn. My dog."

"Why'd you name her Madalynn?"

"It was the first name that popped in my head when I saw her."

"Wanna hang?" He immediately asked.

"Oh, I cant. I've got to get with my friends."

"Boyfriend?"

"Nope. Friends."

"Perfect."

"Perfect?"

"I've got to get home too," he said.

"Girlfriend?" I asked before realizing what just came out of my mouth. *Oh my goodness, Jasmine.*

He smiled, "Girlfriend? No. Best friend. And I stink. Here. Put your number in my phone."

"Sure."

I took his phone from him and saved my number. I felt the redness filling in the blush areas of my makeup-less cheeks. *Get it together, Jasmine.* I made it a point to hand him his phone back and close my door immediately after. He gave me a blank stare through my window, smiled, and walked to his car.

    I pulled out all cool like. No big deal. He turned the same way. No big deal. I turned left. He turned left. I drove past ten blocks. I counted. He also drove past all ten blocks. No big deal. I turned right. He turned right. *What the?* Okay. Maybe he's not that cute. More like creepy. Boys are so stupid. I got to my road and turned left. He kept going. Whew. Okay, maybe he's not a creep.

    My phone buzzed. I looked at it. "Dude." From an unknown number. I sat my phone down and kept driving up my hill. I swear I could still hear his car. *Stop it, Jasmine.*

    I pulled up to my apartment and quickly made it upstairs and inside to get Madalynn and let her out. I wondered who messaged me. Let's be honest. I wondered if it was Jon. I hadn't heard from anyone yet and it was about time to get the "let's go out" text from one of my girls.

    I grabbed Madalynn and started walking down the stairs and began to text the number back. I heard a phone go off right as I pushed send. I looked up. It was Jon.

"Dude," he said, "We're neighbors. And this must be Madalynn."

"I'm not going to lie; I thought you were following me." I said trying to keep my cool.

"Maybe I was."

"Were you?" I was confused.

"Was I?"

I rolled my eyes in response to his sarcasm.

"Can I walk Madalynn with you?"

"Sure," I said.

"I hate that word." He answered.

"Yeah, me too." I agreed.

"So, where are you going tonight?" He asked. "Where do you go? What do you do? How do you know Alex?"

"Alex?" I interrupted.

"Yeah, Alex from the restaurant."

"I figured that's which Alex. Why him?"

"He's my bro," he answered as he flipped his hair to the side.

"Oh. Cool. School for us. I'm closer to Scott. Well, we're close but not close."

"I see. I understand. She's so good!"

"Who?" I asked.

"Madalynn!"

"Oh, yeah. Madalynn."

"And beautiful!" he said as he knelt down and started massaging her the same way I had been right before.

"Dude. Don't even."

"What?" he asked.

"Madalynn is the goofiest looking dog you've ever seen. She has an under bite for days and the most jacked up teeth."

"You're right." He chuckled, "I was just about to ask if she's had braces before. She's beautiful."

"Want to see where I live?" he asked.

"Yeah," I answered without a thought.

Did you just say that out loud Jasmine?

"Yeah," I belted out.

"I know. You just said that. Bring Madalynn." He smiled and turned away.

"Definitely." I answered. "I wouldn't come if she couldn't."

"I like that," he said as he turned back around and held his hand out towards me for a second before lowering it down to Madalynn.

Sure enough his building was on the neighboring street. I was waiting for him to say he was just kidding. He wasn't just kidding.

There was his black Mustang. I followed him up the stairs.

"Your dog loves me."

"No, she just goes where I go."

"Yeah, yeah."

We walked in and I immediately thought it was adorable how what one would call boyish the apartment was. The kitchen was simple with few decorations. There was an oversized beanbag in front of the television that sat in front of an oversized entertainment center. I honestly do not remember the bedrooms which is weird for me to think about now. I'm one of those I'll just wait in the living room kind of people.

"You hungry?" he politely asked.

"No, I ate at the restaurant."

"Oh, yeah, you were eating Travis's brother's chicken strips."

"Oh yeah? You watched me eat?" I laughed.

"Well, I guess, yeah. Yes I did."

Silence. *What do I say? Why isn't he talking? He watched me eat?* I thought to myself.

"Cool if I shower right quick?" he startled my thoughts.

"Sure." I hesitated, "I mean, yeah, I guess. I'll actually probably head back and shower."

"Just wait right here," he asked, "Please?"

"Okay," I agreed.

Another awkward stare. *What's going on in his head?* He then gave me a huge smile. *Is he messing with me? Can he hear me thinking? STOP IT, JASMINE.*

Ten minutes passed in what seemed like two. He came out only in his towel. I did everything I could to avoid looking at him. *What an idiot.* His hair was surfer boy wet and still dripping.

I immediately turned away and he laughed. "Sorry, I forgot my phone and I've got to see what time my bro is off work tonight."

He walked past and as he passed I noticed he had a koi fish that covered half of his arm and matching star tattoos above the back of each elbow.

Sexy. STOP IT, JASMINE.

He returned to his room and came out five minutes later wearing a black v-neck and form fitting jeans.

"Wanna hang?" he asked.

I looked down at my black polo and over at Madalynn who as always was looking back at me.

"Sure," I answered, "but I've got to get back home and shower."

"Cool! Let me grab my stuff!" He literally jumped with excitement.

"Oh, no," I quickly responded, "come over in thirty."

"Okay, okay." He agreed.

I wasn't sure what else to say or do so I turned and walked out of his apartment door, back down the stairs, back across the street, back between the two buildings that stood between ours, back across my street, back up my stairs, and back inside my apartment.

Is this really happening? Neighbors? Wild. But that's how my life has always worked. The most ridiculous coincidences.

5

I took the fastest shower I had ever taken before. I was paranoid I'd hear a knock on the door sooner than the thirty minutes I requested were up. An hour passed. *Should I message him?*

All of a sudden there was a knock on the door. I swung it open.

"Hey, girl!" Gio said as she entered my apartment and plopped down on the couch. "That's not what you're wearing, is it?" She looked me up and down. "Got any beer?"

"Yeah, sure, I'm about to change. Check the fridge."

I walked to my room slower than a zombie in case anyone else was about to knock before I made it there. Nothing. I looked at my phone. Nothing. *Stop it, Jasmine.*

"What's going on with you?" Gio asked looking up at me with her eyes bulged. I was never sure if her eyes bulged naturally with her beauty or if it was something she made herself do. I always wondered.

"Nothing." I shrugged. "Grab that six pack and I'll put it in my purse. You driving tonight?"

"Yeah, girl," she answered on her way to my fridge.

We got to Magoos, which was the current hot spot at the time. Still no message from Jon. The night went on just as any other night. It didn't take long for Jon to disappear from my thoughts. But just as fast as my mind rid itself of him, he was back in it. I looked at my phone. Three missed calls. All Jon. Did this dude just call me three times in a row?

"What's up?" I text him.

11:12 Jon: I'm so sorry. My bro had issues with his girl and I had to be there.
11:14 Me: No worries.
11:15 Jon: I noticed you weren't home.
11:30 Me: Really? My car is home.
11:31 Jon: I knocked.
11:31 Jon: And called.
11:32 Jon: A couple times.
11:38 Me: A few lol
11:39 Jon: Yes, a few. Where are you?
11:45 Me: Dancing.
11:46 Jon: I want to dance with you. Where you at?

11:50 Me: I'm at Magoos. I don't dance with guys. Sorry to disappoint
11:51 Jon: Can I come get you?
11:51 Me: Yes.
11:54 Me: ?
12:07 Me: ??

"Get off your phone!" Gio yelled over the music as she grabbed my arm and pulled me to the bar handing me a shot.
"I'm tired. I might leave."
"How are you leaving girl? I'm not leaving. We aren't leaving yet." There were those bulging eyes again.
"I have a ride girl, no worries."
"Who?!" Bulging eyes in full effect.
"Oh, just a new friend from work. His name is-".
"His?" I'm convinced her eyes were popped out of socket.
"Yes, Gio. Just a nice guy. He lives in the same apartments as me. His name is Jon."
"Oh girl. Cheers to no more JJ!"
I almost dropped my shot. "Gio!"
She had a laugh that matched her eyes and beauty.

"Cheers to a safe ride home!" I said after realizing she already took her shot.

12:28 Me: ??
12:32 Jon: Here.

I hugged and kissed Gio goodbye and grabbed my purse.
Clank, clank. *Score.*
I got to the door and opened it to Jon's car parked right out front. I got in trying to poise myself as soberly as possible.
Clank, clank.
"What's that?" Jon looked at my purse.
"Beer."
"You carry beer in your purse in the bar?"
"Some say it's crazy. I say it's genius."
He laughed. "Are you drunk?"
"A bit." I was trying so hard not to look at him.
"You're wearing makeup."
Goodness he made my cheeks fill with heat more than anyone I've ever been around. I laughed and opened a beer.
"Is this okay with you?" I asked after I took a drink.

"Whatever you want." He smiled and turned the music up and didn't say another word until we pulled up to my apartment.

"Oh shit, are you hungry?" He asked as soon as he turned his engine off.

"I've got food upstairs. Are you hungry?"

"Nah. You mind if I come up?"

"No. You might get bored, though."

"I'm sure you'll be entertaining enough," he said as he was getting out of the car.

We got inside and I let Madalynn out of her bathroom bedroom.

"Want me to take her out for you?" he offered.

"Yes, please."

"Come on, Madalynn!" They both walked out of the door. *Perfect.*

I had my face washed and my favorite athletic shorts on by the time he made it back. Surely if I had my face washed and was all tomboyed out he wouldn't be interested in me. Surely he wasn't interested in me anyways and just thought it'd be nice to have a friend who lived close by. Surely he was just bored and wanted someone to hang out with.

Stop it, Jasmine.

I jumped when they walked through the living room door.

"I'm sorry!" he said laughing. "She's such a good dog!"

"Mhmm," I agreed.

"Can I have a tour? Can I sit? Should I stand?" He didn't move from the doorway.

I laughed, "Nope!"

He laughed.

"I'm just kidding. This is my living room. I got my couch from Alex."

"Oh, I know."

"Okay. And this is my tiny television."

"Nice, nice. Where are your curtains?" he asked.

"That's a good question. However, I've never really felt the need for any."

"Whatever floats your boat," he laughed. "What are all of these pictures?"

He was now in the kitchen looking at the collage of pictures on my fridge.

"These are actually all old pictures. I call it my flashback area." I pointed and "introduced" him to all of my lifelong friends and informed him of their current status in my life.

We made it down the hall and into my bedroom.

"And this is my room," I said nervously as he walked in.

I had a queen box spring beneath a mattress that was covered in a hot pink sheet. My comforter was oversized and black.

"I'm not much of a bed maker."

"I noticed."

He looked at all of my random clutter on my vanity and wandered over to my closet.

"Wow, what's all of this?" he asked, looking at my closet wall that I had decorated with art and poems I saved from friends over the years.

"Well, I think it's really special when someone draws or writes something for me. So I save almost everything like that."

"This is amazing," he said and proceeded to bend in and read an apology poem Huddleston had written me five years before.

I had my burgundy colored wooden beaded necklaces hanging on my vanity. He grabbed one.

"This is so cool! I love it. Can I have it?"

"No, Jon." I laughed. "Put it back."

"Hey, I need to run and get my charger. Unless you have an iPhone charger?" he asked after scoping out the rest of my room.

I watched him as if he was about to steal something.

"I do not. Good thing we're neighbors."

He smiled. "I'll be right back." He walked out of my apartment with no more than that. He left his phone on my couch.

Hmm. JJ never left his phone in the same room as me.

Ten minutes passed. So I thought. I opened my eyes to the morning sun gleaming through the blinds of my curtainless window. I was on my couch where Jon had left me. Only to realize he must've come back. His phone was gone. And so was he.

    The next three weeks were nothing but fun. Life was good. At first it seemed weird how I was with Jon most days and almost every night. We had kissed a few times. Always out of nowhere, usually when he became overly excited about something or when I couldn't handle reacting to the way he looked at me.

    We were inseparable. It was refreshing having a friend to rely on other than the normal let's-get-drunk friends I met up with every weekend. I'm not complaining about those friends. Maybe I should re-word it. It was gratifying having a friend day in and day out rather than just when it was time to party. Mind you, I have zero complaints about partying. Maybe what I'm just trying to say is: It was nice having Jon.

I've always had guy friends. But those turned into boyfriends usually or weird crushes that ended after awkward kisses or hook ups. Jon was different. And Alex came with Jon.

Jon was younger than Alex and me. Alex was my age, yet had his shit together more than any other twenty-three-year-old I knew. He had his own one bedroom apartment above an abandoned store. It was superb and clean and had the tallest windows I've ever seen. He had just gotten a new couch since he recently sold me his. He had a big screen. I found myself lying on his couch every time I went over there with Jon.

He had the most interesting choices of food. I don't want to say it's because he's Russian, but it was Russian food. If it wasn't just me and Jon, it was me, Jon, and Alex. He's the kind of guy that people get to know and come up with those corny sayings like, "You know a good guy when you see one." Alex was definitely that guy.

His parents lived across the way. His mother had a deep Russian accent. I only ventured over there about three times with Jon and Alex and each time she offered me food. She didn't smile much, but each time our eyes met she gave me a pleasant smile. I loved when she talked to Alex in Russian.

Normally I wouldn't be able to describe one's bedroom. I can barely describe Alex's other than you walked through it to get to the window that leads to the roof. Right outside his window was a rather large, flat area covered in what looked like black asphalt. You could fry an egg out there on a hot day. That must be why I thought it'd be a great idea to lay out there to get rid of my tan lines. Jon thought it was a great idea, too. Jon thought all my ideas were great.

We got out on the roof and laid out some towels. Alex wasn't joining us. It was too hot and he wanted to count his money or something like that. Jon laid his towel a bit behind me and sprung out. His body was so long. He used two towels.

"I wish I would have grabbed two towels."

"Here, take mine," he said leaping right up. "I'll go grab another one."

He threw it at me and disappeared through the window before I could tell him I'd be okay with just one.

"It's so hot out here. I'm going to untie my back strap and let the sun get to work," I said looking at him assuming he could read my mind not to look at me so I could untie it.

"Don't mind me," he grinned.

I untied my strap and laid down on my stomach with my hands pillowing my head.

"I'm going to try and fall asleep."

"Good luck," he answered. "I feel like we're giving ourselves free tickets to skin cancer."

I laughed. I felt like I was melting. I felt pretty uncomfortable knowing how much I was sweating with Jon lying there. I turned my head and looked over at him. He was staring at me.

"Why are you staring at me?"

"I can't help it."

And for the first time since we started hanging out I was lost for words and couldn't break the silence with a flirty friendly kiss because I was stuck topless unable to move. Of course he didn't say anything. I glared at him and he looked at me. I felt as if a million thoughts went from my head to his and vice versa. I couldn't take it. I closed my eyes. He won.

He hopped back up. "We can't lay out here and die and if we don't go in that's what we're going to do. Need help with your top?"

"I've got it. You just go in. And don't look back, Jon, I mean it."

He grabbed his towels, went to the window, stopped in his tracks, and turned around. He came back and kissed me right in the middle of my sweaty back before he disappeared back through the window. I'll never forget feeling as though my heart went backwards through my body to meet his lips on my spine.

7

Jon and I left Alex's apartment and came back to mine.

"Well, I'm going to shower," I said as I unlocked my apartment. "I don't care if you chill here, but I might take a while. I'm feeling gross and still sweaty."

"Want me to walk Madalynn for you?"

"She's not here. My mom is watching her for me today."

If you didn't know us, you'd assumed we lived there together by how comfortable he was in my home and how much he knew his way around my kitchen and how he'd tidy up after himself.

"Can I shower with you?" his voice cracked when he asked.

"Are you serious? Jon, you're crazy." I grabbed my favorite high school basketball tee and black shorts.

"About you," he said in a goofy low voice.

"Good one."

"Come on. I won't bother you and I swear I won't touch you."

"Okay, fine. But! The lights have to be off and you can't touch me."

"Deal."

"I've got to get in first and then I'll say when it's okay."

"Okay."

"Jon I swear if you touch me or turn on the lights I will punch you and I swear I can punch like a dude."

"Okay, I swear! Geez."

"Geez? I'm about to take a shower with you. Don't geez me."

I went into the bathroom and gazed in the mirror a bit. There I was, cheeks red from today's cooking session in the sun. I put my shower cap on. I took my shower cap off. I put it back on. I removed my bikini and continued to stare. *Surely he's seen way better figured girls than me naked. Sexy girls. He won't see me anyways.* I started the water and set the temperature a little hotter than normal.

"Okay, I'm ready!" I called after three failed attempts of allowing the words to escape my mouth. "Jon?"

"I'm coming, I'm coming. Why are you rushing me?" He laughed. He stepped in the shower.

Wow, was he naked already?

"Alright. I already basically washed everything so you can have the water for a bit. I'll stand over here."

"Give me your hands," he said as he reached for my arms. It was pitch black. He put his hands on my shoulders and worked them down my arms to my hands and guided me to switch places with him.

I had never taken a shower with anyone, let alone let anyone other than a boyfriend touch me. Nervous was an understatement. I was both terrified and excited at the same time. I want to describe my feelings as love, but it wasn't love because I've only known Jon for what? A month?

"Are you not going to talk?" he asked while I assume his face was in the water.

"Umm... well. Need help with your back?"

"That'd be amazing," he answered while handing me a washcloth and holding it on my chest allowing me time to find it in the dark.

"Want me to wash yours?" He offered after I had finished.

"Nope."

"Well, can I kiss you? Would one consider this romantic? This seems pretty romantic to me even though-"

I'm not sure how I found his lips in the dark but I did and I kissed him before he could finish his sentence. I could feel his smile forming between kisses and he pulled me by my shoulders closer to him beneath the cascading water all while keeping our bodies apart.

"What's that noise?" he asked as soon as I joined him closer under the water.

"Oh umm... it's my shower cap."

He laughed.

I laughed. I got out of the shower and grabbed my towel and turned the light on before exiting.

Jon took about another fifteen minutes in the shower. During that time I got dressed and applied a fresh coat of mascara. I stood in the mirror paying more attention to my hair than normal. I spent a good three minutes reminding myself I was single and Jon hadn't touched any off limits part of my body. That it was possible for this guy to just enjoy my company and like all my jokes and even my loudness and annoying habit of babbling until I confessed I forgot the point of whatever story I was trying to tell.

Of course he wanted to take a shower with me. He's a guy. I'm a girl. He's probably taken a hundred showers with a hundred girls. Stop it, Jasmine.

I heard the bathroom door open. I sat down quickly on my bed. Then stood up. Then sat down. He rounded the corner. He was still in his towel.

"Oh. Umm... You can get dressed in here."

I stood back up and started through the doorway. He grabbed my hand as I walked by and used his other hand to cup my face. *Surely he isn't going to kiss me.* I felt a little awkward as I smiled and tried to continue out of the door. He pulled me to the bed. *Stop it, Jasmine.* He started kissing me. I couldn't close my eyes. *Stop it, Jasmine.* He used his kissing to push me back to where I was fully lying down and he was on top of me. I've never kissed him lying down before. *Stop it, Jasmine.* He pulled my comforter over him. His body was completely covering mine but he somehow managed to not make me feel smooshed at all.

We finally took a break from kissing. He stared at me. I awkwardly attempted to take my shirt off. He helped. He playfully kissed me first on my chest and then back to my lips and then down to my navel and back to my lips. *Try not to act too into it.* I couldn't stay still. I couldn't take my eyes off of his chest or his smile or his hair or the way the muscles in his arms defined each time he moved his body to hold his weight off of me.

He disappeared under the comforter and removed my shorts slowly. He kissed his way up my legs, over my panties, up past my navel, over my chest, and back to my lips. He put his hand between my legs and started tugging to remove my panties. I positioned myself to allow him to do so and I could feel him smile while we kissed. The only thing between us now was his towel. He also wasn't protecting me from his weight anymore. *Stop it, Jasmine.*

"You want me to stop?" he asked after letting go of my bottom lip.

"No."

8

I woke up the next morning with Jon in my bed. He had slept with me before, but the night before was our first time *sleeping* together. He was smiling in his sleep. Could he be dreaming of the best twenty minutes I've ever had nine hours ago? Then he winced.

"Well, good morning Jasmine." He opened his eyes and immediately greeted me with a smile.

"You hungry?" I asked.

"Always."

I got up and took Madalynn out on a walk without giving him an invite. I smiled the entire time. The crazy lady neighbor downstairs told me I looked like I had had an amazing cup of coffee. *If only she knew.* Madalynn kept looking at me while she walked. Did Madalynn know? *Stop it, Jasmine.*

After the walk I returned to my apartment. Jon was still in my bed. I poured us each a bowl of cereal and cup of chocolate milk.

"Oh, how sweet," he greeted me laughing as I walked in my room. "Breakfast in bed."

"Sure." I rolled my eyes, "What's that?"

He had one of my notebooks from college opened and was going to town on the paper with a blue ink pen. "For you. For your closet." He ripped the page out and handed it to me. It was a sketch of Madalynn.

"Annnnnd I love you!" I immediately grabbed some scissors from my vanity and started cutting around Madalynn's body.

"It's about time."

"What?" I looked up from my cutting job.

"You love me. It's about time."

"Jon, shut up."

"I wanted to tell you last night but figured it'd be too cliché. First in the shower before your shower cap interrupted and then after... you know. Right before you fell asleep. I whispered it to you and you smiled so I assumed you heard me."

"I didn't hear anything and you don't love me, Jon. You just like me very much." I grabbed some tape out of my main junk drawer and added Madalynn's picture to my closet art collection. "It's perfect. Thank you."

"Anything for you, Jasmine. I love you."

I turned around. He was standing there giving me crazy eyes over the rim of his chocolate milk.

"You can shut up now."

"Hey, you said it first."

The rest of the day he told me he loved me. If I didn't love hearing him say it so much I would have been annoyed. If it was anyone else I would have been annoyed.

...

He, Alex, and I ended up at some random barbeque my parents invited me to. It was hot as ever but my hair was having a hard time staying down so I wore a stocking cap. *He must love me if he doesn't care that I'm wearing a stocking cap in eighty degree weather.*

He followed me to the bathroom and pushed his way in as I was trying to close the door for some privacy. He kissed me. I noticed he had one of my wooden necklace on.

"I love you, Jasmine."

"I'm not going to be your girlfriend, Jon."

He kissed me again.

"You will."

"No, I won't. I can't."

He kissed me again. "You still love me."

"It's been weeks, Jon."

"I started loving you three weeks ago Jasmine. Maybe four. Who's counting?"

"You're so lame. I've got to pee. I'll be taking my necklace back by the way."

He backed up to the door and started to back himself out slowly.

I couldn't wait so I started to pull my pants down and sit on the toilet. He stopped and watched.

"Seriously?"

He waited.

"I love you, Jon."

"I knew it," he smiled, "Isn't this romantic?"

"Jon!"

After I had finished and cleaned up I found him outside beating my father in a game of horse shoes while my mother cheered him on.

I wrote JJ that night when I was home alone. I told him about Jon. Not about Jon, but about our friendship and hanging out. I knew it'd probably aggravate him. But he was in there and I was out here. I was as honest as I could be. I loved JJ. No matter how bad he was for me, I could never and would never hide the way I felt about him. No matter what my family, friends, and now Jon said about him. I couldn't deny my feelings for that idiot. However, my letters did start to have more pauses between sending them.

The next day was Monday. Jon didn't come in to the restaurant because he wasn't feeling well. I missed him. I hated that he was sick. His mom lived about forty minutes away in the next town, his bro was working a double that day, and his sister didn't live nearby. He was alone and I know how much I hate being alone and need my mother when I'm sick. Before I left work that night I grabbed a few pouches of instant green tea for him that he was always drinking at work.

I got home early, right at nine. Savannah's had been dead. Jon text and asked if I minded for him to come get me sick. I laughed and replied with a come on over. I picked up some Chinese on my way home and he fake vomited when I offered him my leftovers.

"I feel like I have a worm trying to come up my throat and out of my nose," he said mid fake dry heave.

"That's gross," I said as I grabbed my purse. "Oh, here, I have something for you." I grabbed a packet of tea.

"You got this for me?" his eyes were big and he looked in shock as if I handed him a twenty dollar bill.

"Um.. yeah, there's a few in there if you ever want them."

"I can't believe you have something in your house for me."

I thought he was joking. "You're a nerd. It's just tea. And it was free."

"This means so much to me. You have no idea."

Is he being serious?

He held the packet in his hand and stared at it with a smile. *What's going on here?*

He opened up my cabinet and saw the rest and closed it. "Seriously Jasmine, thank you. I love you."

"Love you too, Jon," I said with a laugh.

I still have one of those packets to this day.

9

The next week went by quick. Work then work then hang out with Jon then sleep then work. Wednesday he, Alex, and I had the night off so after I got off at the preschool we went to a school yard and played some basketball.

"Jasmine was an all-star in school, y'know?" Alex said to Jon as he threw me the ball.

"Yeah, she told me," Jon panted from exhaustion.

"Is there anything she hasn't told you?"

"I'm sure," Jon laughed as he got my rebound and shot and missed."

"You two are practically married. It's time to start planning."

"Um, no." I had the ball and made my shot. I looked at Jon. He glared back and looked upset.

...

He had been asking me about us being together, being official, and being boyfriend and girlfriend. I told him I couldn't. There's no way I could live with breaking his heart and that's exactly what would happen.

JJ would get out of prison and I would choose him and I would hurt Jon. He insured me that wouldn't happen. That one, by then I'd be so in love with Jon, JJ wouldn't phase me, and two, there's no way he would allow me to get back with JJ after he learned what JJ had done to me and how most of our five years together were spent.

"You don't deserve that," he'd say.

"It was both of us," I'd rebuttal.

"I'm going to show you how special you are," he'd say.

"You already have," I'd reply, "but we just can't be together."

We'd fight about it. We'd make up. It was an ongoing battle. Our personal battle. Because we had personal battles. I never had a friendship like this. He felt the same.

"You know, you can get a girlfriend and I'd have to be okay with it," I'd tell him. That always pissed him off the most.

"Oh, and you can get a boyfriend and I'd kill him," he'd say. "You're mine. Not JJ's, not anyone else's, but mine. And I'm yours."

...

Jon threw the ball over Alex's head and Alex had to go fetch it.

"Tabitha likes me," he said as he walked towards me.

"Not her, Jon. You can't date her."

"I wouldn't. I think she takes my politeness as flirting."

"If she thinks you're flirting, you're probably flirting," I laughed, "But no, not her."

"So you care? Are you jealous?"

Alex ran back and did a layup. I ignored Jon's question.

We finished up our ball session and got in Jon's car. I thought about Tabitha the entire way home. I was upset. Tabitha and I had a rocky past and not the best memories when it came to guys. I felt she betrayed me in a lot of ways and although I had forgiven her, in my heart Jon was way too good for her. There's no way I would let that happen. There's no way I'd let her hurt him.

"You coming to my place?" Alex asked me as we pulled away.

"No, I've got to get some shopping done. Alone."

Jon looked back at me.

"Okay," he said, "I'll drop you off."

"Thanks." I looked down at my phone.

I wanted to text Tabitha. Mark my territory.

Stop it, Jasmine.

The guys dropped me off. I got out of the car and half assed said goodbye. I was throwing a fit. I was irate. And the confusing part was I didn't understand why I was so upset. I knew I couldn't be with Jon, but I also knew what it was like to have an ex that I loved hate me because of me choosing JJ. I had a couple of exes hate me because of JJ. I couldn't bear to have Jon end up hating me as well.

There was no way I could let Tabitha be the girl Jon gave his attention to, though. He was too perfect for her. But that wasn't even the issue. All I kept thinking was *he's mine.* But he wasn't mine. No matter how much he'd say it. He wasn't mine and I wasn't his. Not officially. And it was my fault. My choice. Just. No. Not Tabitha. I knew what I had to do.

The next night at the restaurant I told Tabitha how I felt.

"Hey girl. So um, Jon said he thinks you like him or something like that."

"Girl, please," she smiled. "He's sexy and sweet but way too young for my liking."

"Tabitha, he's as old as your ex." I laughed, "But anyways, I just want you to know I like him."

"Oh?" she looked at me wittingly and then continued to walk. "Okay. That changes things."

"Yeah, I didn't want us having any issues, not that we would, but you know what I'm saying."

"Yeah. What about JJ? You finally smarten up and kick him to the curb?"

"I'm trying. Jon is changing a lot of how I feel about everything."

She stopped and put her hands on my shoulders. "Good. Jon is good. You deserve good, Jasmine. You deserve better than good. You don't have to worry about me. If you're telling me you have feelings for Jon then you must have some pretty legit feelings for Jon."

"Thanks, girl. We'll see." And that was that.

...

After work Jon came over as usual.
"So you talked to Tabitha."
"I did."
"So you love me."
"I do."

"She said that if you approached her to tell her you like me then you must like me and that I shouldn't mess it up."

"I'm the one who is messing all of this up."

"No, Jasmine. You're not messing anything up. Your realness with me is one of the reasons I love you."

"Let's chill out on saying love."

"Really?"

"I mean, yeah, Jon. What are we even doing?"

"Living life to the fullest?"

"You're so corny."

"That's why you love me."

"Let's party tomorrow. Can we? I need a night out."

"You're always out, but okay," he agreed.

"I'm in love with you, Jon."

"What? Really? Jasmine."

"Okay? I said it. And I want to chill out on it. It's confusing. I'm in love with two people. I don't even know how to feel. You're just so... great. And I feel that I'm not. Because of JJ. I feel like... lost."

"He's not even here, Jasmine."

"I know but, I don't know. I don't know why I feel how I feel. But I'm not going to lie to you about it."

"And that's why I'm in love with you. We don't have to say it and we can do and handle it however you want. You're my best friend. I'm here for you."

I kissed him.

He kissed me back harder.

"You staying here tonight?"

"I've got plans with the bro. Tomorrow though, me and you."

"Alright. I'll see you at work."

He kissed me again before he left, "See you."

I took a hot shower and cried myself to sleep. I couldn't tell if it was over JJ or Jon or both. I just cried myself unconscious.

For crying myself to sleep the night before, Friday I woke up in the best mood. I grabbed a white mocha from Starbucks on the way to work and had a smile on my face the entire morning. On my break I wrote JJ.

JJ,
Things are wild out here. Hope it's not too wild in there. I think I might start writing less. I'm going to keep this short because honestly I shouldn't be writing you anyways. Right? Out here making moves on my own has me looking at life differently. I wish things were different. But they aren't. You've only got a couple months left in there, so I think I'm going to slow down until you get out. Get my head right and ready. I saw your mom the other day. It's weird that she's in a house you won't be seeing. Everything is weird. Just wanted to shoot you some lines. Sorry about the long pause. I don't want to say I've been too busy, but with two jobs and living on my own, time has been flying by. Hope it's flown by for you as well. Don't be mad about me taking a break from writing. I've got too much on my mind. Life is a blur.

Yours Always,
Jas

  I put the letter in an envelope, stamped it, and ran it to the post office down the street. I told myself that was closure. I knew he'd be upset, but I was at a place with myself that I was okay with that. I had enabled him to still have me for almost his entire year in there. I didn't want to anymore. At least for the time being.

The rest of my day went by swiftly. I made the kids laugh all day as usual and kept my co-workers smiling as well. I was really feeling good and like myself. I sent Jon a text.

3:48 Me: Jon.
3:49 Jon: I've been waiting to hear from you. What's up? You ok? We are first out tonight.
4:02 Me: I want you. Let's have fun tonight.
4:12 Jon: What you mean you want me? Of course.
4:13 Me: See you in a bit.
4:15 Jon: See you xo

My boss stopped me on my way out of the door at 4:30.

"Jasmine. You're glowing." She had a strange look on her face.

"I'm just feeling really good. I think I'm in love. Ha-ha."

"What? With that Jon kid? Jasmine!"

"Ha-ha. I think so. Who knows. I'm just.... Happy. And it's nice."

"Good. Stop being so stuck on JJ. I'm happy to see you so happy."

"Have you ever felt in love with a friend but not enough to allow it to happen? Like, I don't want to hurt him."

"Just keep being you, Jasmine." And before we could finish she was called down the hallway to assist another teacher.

"Have a good weekend, Megan!" I shouted as she walked away.

"You too, dear."

I got home, changed out of my red polo into my black polo, and headed to the restaurant early to help with the prep.

"Christinnnnaaaaaaa!" Rosita cheered as I walked in.

"Rossiiittaaaaaaaa!" I cheered back.

"What's going on with you and Jon?" she asked.

"Oh, you know, just a couple of best friends trying not to fall in love."

She laughed. "You two are hilarious. I love you."

"Love you too, beautiful."

Jon came in shortly after. He looked like he had showered right before work. He had gotten a haircut, too.

"I just showered," he said as he passed me.

"I can tell. Your hair is shorter too."

"You noticed?"

"I mean, well yes, I see you every day."

"I was tripping out on feeling my cut hair down my shirt, so I had to shower before I came in. You like it?"

"It looks the same."

"Then how did you notice it was cut?"

"Well, because it's shorter."

"So, it's the same but shorter?"

"It looks good, Jon. You look good."

He kissed me on the cheek and then went to help Rosita carry the ice bucket.

The night flew by and before I knew it I had eighty dollars cash and was ready to clock out. Jon finished up right as I did and we walked out together.

"You still want me?" He stopped me right before we walked out of the door.

"Huh?" I played dumb.

"Come on, Jasmine. You've had me excited all day."

"Come over when you're ready," I said as we continued to walk to our cars. "I'll drive tonight. I told Tierrah we'd be by before we go out."

"She coming tonight?"

"No. She doesn't feel like it. Everyone else is, though."

He walked me to my car and opened my door for me. "I've wanted you all day. You better not be playing with me."

"I wrote JJ and made closure. Well, I told him I wasn't going to write as much even though I haven't been writing much anyways."

"Oh. Wow. You okay?"

"I'm great actually. See you in a bit."

"See you," he replied as he closed my door.

11

Something had come over me. I don't know if it was the sense of closure I felt with JJ, feeling love for Jon, or what it was. I smiled to myself the entire time in the shower.

...

The way my brain works is about a million topics and scenarios play out in my head that are very rarely even remotely related and when I snap out of it I can rarely put the pieces together. But the happiness I feel while "gone" is more than real.

Sometimes I find myself so happy with my surroundings I feel as if I'm in a movie. Even the colors seem different, or seem to pop. I tell myself it's because I have the eyes of an artist or a high leveled imagination. I don't know how else to explain it. My brain never rests.

I think this is why I was able to pick what I dreamt about when I was a child. I had two favorite dreams I'd always bring myself to.

The one I would go to most was a hidden culvert behind one of my grandfather's old salvage yards. I'd always imagine walking the half mile across the field of grass that always went right over my knees, just long enough to tickle my fingertips as I crossed it. I'd walk to an area that only had a few feet of trees and when I'd cross through the culvert there would be zebras and monkeys and giraffes and whatever other animal that would show up. I couldn't talk to the animals but they'd always greet me as if they missed me while I was gone.

I also had another favorite dream where I could go out to my grandmother and grandfather's backyard, hold a stick up in the air as I climbed onto the dog house, and take off in flight. That was always so fun.

When I'd go to these dreams I'd always know I was dreaming, but I couldn't think too much about it otherwise I would wake up. Aside from a few reoccurring nightmares, my dreams when I was a child were one of my favorite places to be.

To this day at times I can still tell when I'm in a dream. It's an unbelievable feeling. I wake up sometimes upset because I was having so much fun.

...

I'm one hell of a daydreamer who often has to bring myself back to reality from fantasy land. The hot water running out in the shower brought me back that night.

One of my favorite things about Jon was no matter what I'd wear; he'd say I looked great. I've always just worn whatever I wanted without caring or having much thought about what anyone else thought, but at the same time I was always aware it wasn't always as stylish or girly as the norm. While my friends rocked Hollister, I'd have my leggings underneath my basketball shorts. However, that night I wanted to be cuter than usual.

I slid my new skinny jeans on with a black tank and my semi worn out three quarter sleeved turquoise and burgundy plaid light weight jacket. I put on matching eye shadow that I quickly washed off. I perfected my hair after a ten minute debate with myself on whether to wear my Converse that didn't quite match or my black flats that did.

"Hello?" Jon announced as he walked through my door without knocking.

I slid into my closet.

"Jasmine?" I could hear him walking down the hallway. "Madalynn? Where's your Madre?"

He entered my room and Madalynn walked right up to me and started wagging her tail.

"Good girl, baby!" he laughed.

"Damn dog, Madalynn!" I nudged her to the side, "Good thing he isn't a murderer!"

"Can't get mad that she loves me and listens to me so well." He looked at her and started scratching behind her ears. "You love your step daddy Jon, don't you?"

"You are an idiot. Stop." I rolled my eyes.

"Come on!" he laughed.

"No."

He had on his black v-neck shirt that looked rather new and some jeans and shoes I've never seen before.

"Do you buy black v-necks in bulk?"

"Yes. Are you making fun of me?"

"No! You look good in them. Just asking out loud finally."

He laughed. "Do you ever match?"

"Jon!"

"What?" He held up his hands.

I kicked my shoes off and slid on my flats.

He smiled, "I was just asking out loud finally."

"Let's go." I grabbed my phone off of the charger. "I still want to go by Tierrah's first."

"Oh, fun! I'll drive. I know you said you would, but I just want to tonight." He swung his keys around his finger.

"Good. I've already had three beers."

12

We were halfway to Tierrah's when he grabbed my hand.

"I really like holding your hand," he said all romantic like at a stop sign.

I giggled a little, "I like you holding my hand."

"We should just be together."

"We are together, Jon."

"Seriously, Jasmine. Let's be together for real."

"This is real. Why mess it up?"

"It won't mess up."

"But JJ."

"Fuck JJ. I'm sick of 'but JJ'. JJ isn't here."

"He will be."

"Bullshit!" He took his hands off the steering wheel. "So what am I supposed to do?" he continued. "Just wait around and see what happens? Put my life on hold?"

"What's gotten into you, Jon?"

"I love you, Jasmine."

"And I love you, but by all means if your heart or brain is pulling you somewhere else then you need to just go. I already told you that you can do whatever."

"Oh, but not Tabitha?"

"Seriously, Jon?"

"Yes, I'm serious. I just want to have you."

"You do have me. Can we just go? I don't want to do this." I opened a beer. We started moving forward and he slammed on the brakes as a car passed in front of us honking.

"Jon!"

"It came out of nowhere!"

We sat in the middle of the road.

"Drive," I said as I wiped up some beer that spilled out when we stopped.

"No."

"What? We almost just died and you want to sit here in the road? Drive!"

"Tell me no one else has you."

"That'd be lying."

"Say it."

"You have me."

"Say no one else." He had a look in his eyes I've never seen.

"Jon."

"Say it!"

"No one else has me. Can we go now? There's a car coming."

He pulled out of the intersection and stopped again.

"Jon, we have to go."

"We should have a baby."

"Are you kidding me right now?" I laughed and choked on my beer.

"My family has money," he continued, "We'd be set."

"You're crazy, Jon."

"I'm serious, Jasmine."

"No."

"We'd be so happy." He took my hand again.

"Jon, we're kids. You're a kid. We can't. Just drive."

"I'm serious," he said as he put his car back into drive.

"Yeah, I can tell. Seriously crazy."

He finally pulled off after we let the third pissed-off car drive around us.

"What's gotten into you, Jon?"

"I don't know. I've just got a lot on my mind lately."

"Obviously."

"I'm sorry." He shook his head. "I've never done this before."

"You're overthinking. Just be yourself and enjoy life. And I'll be right next to you for as long as you want me to be doing the same."

13

We pulled up in front of Tierrah's house.
...
    Tierrah was my lifelong best friend. I can't exactly count back how many years it's been, but when people ask now I say about fifteen years. Which I believe is accurate now that I'm thirty. She called me her "day1" today.
    I was often asked if our friendship was based on the fact that we were two out of the less than fifteen black kids in our school that just happened to be in the same grade. That's the kind of questions you get asked when you live in a town where you're one of the only black kids growing up. But no. We were best friends because we were so much alike. Of course we had just as many differences as similarities, but we both looked at the importance of life the same way. We both were always ready to have a good time with whoever was willing to embark on one of our random adventures. A lot of times it was just me and her of course, but we also had our separate friends. No matter the situation or time that we

would find ourselves apart, nothing ever changed.

Between Jon, two jobs, and life, we didn't see each other on the regular. She had just gotten a house with her younger sister, Brooke, and her close friend, Ken. I'm also more into going out than she ever has been.

To this day I miss us battle rapping victims when the time came. By the way, we still rap at times, and we're good. I also miss the bus rides to and from the track meets and the poops we'd take together before almost every basketball game for four years.

Her family is my second family from her mother to her sisters to her sister's children. Now I miss her. She told me she was going to buy a house for me to rent out today. "Just tryna help my day1's," she said.

...

I started gathering my things.

"What if Tierrah doesn't like me?" Jon asked as he grabbed my hand.

"Just be yourself."

I felt rude rolling my eyes, but sometimes I couldn't take feeling like he didn't know his worth. Sometimes I expected him to think like me.

Ken greeted us at the door. "Well, you look adorable!" She said as she hugged me. "Where are you guys off to?"

"Magoos!" Jon answered with a little more excitement than needed.

"Well, of course. You must be Jon." She offered her hand to him.

He kindly shook it. "Yes! Hello!"

I'm not sure where his perkiness came from, but I found myself giggling.

"And tall!" Ken continued as she shook his hand.

Jon smiled.

"Tierrah is in the bathroom. I've got to get some stuff done in my room right quick. Come let me know before you leave. Nice to meet you, Jon!" Ken walked off and shut herself in her room.

I walked down to Brooke's bedroom.

"Where y'all going tonight? Magoos?" Brooke asked as we entered.

"Yes girl, you coming?"

"Nope. I can't tonight," she said as she turned around to continue straightening her hair.

"Hey, I'm Jon!" He threw himself on her bed. I thought he was going to bounce right off onto the floor.

"Well, okay then." She laughed and looked over at me.

I was relieved to see Jon being his normal yet slightly overly animated self.

"So, this is your new boo thang?" She was going back and forth from me and Jon with her straightener pointed at us.

"Something like that." I laughed.

"Yes, it's true." Jon laughed and closed his eyes.

"It's about time," she continued while making the humping motion with her hips and arms.

"Jasmine?" Tierrah came in and walked into Brooke's bathroom to use the mirror. She looked like she was going somewhere.

"Where are you going? You can't come out with me, but looks like you're about to go hang with someone else."

"Oh, I meant to message you. I'm coming!"

I let out a little squeal.

"Hey, Jon!" she called from the bathroom.

"Hey," he replied.

"You getting wild tonight?"

"I'm driving."

"Boo!" She turned around with her thumb pointed down. "But, thank you!"

"Sure, no problem." He seemed nervous.

As soon as I thought that he rolled off of Brooke's bed.

Tierrah walked out of the bathroom and jogged down the hall.

I looked at Jon and shrugged. I heard her coming back.

"Here." She pointed a beer towards Jon. "Just have a beer."

He nervously grabbed it. "Sure."

"You okay?" She gave him a questioning look.

"Yeah. I'm just tired and my thoughts are all over the place."

"Jasmine will do that to ya!" She laughed and looked at me. "I like your shoes, though! Wake up! Snap out of it! Come with me." She left the room.

He looked at me and we both shrugged.

"Go." I blew him a kiss and waved him on.

Brooke started playing Boo Thang on her phone and moving her hips around.

"You're wild." I almost spit out my beer laughing.

"He seems to really like you."

"Oh yeah?"

"He just stares at you."

"What?" I rolled my eyes and sat on her bed.

"I was watching him! He just watches you. It's cute."

"Interesting," I said as I stood up, trying to hide my smile.

"Mhmm girl," she said as she turned the volume up on her phone and started doing the humping motion again.

"Girl, bye!" I walked out laughing.

14

I found Jon alone in the kitchen.

"I think she approves," he said as I walked in.

"Approves?" I gave him a puzzled look.

"Yeah. Likes me."

"Yeah, sure. You're weird, Jon. Everyone will like you. Everyone likes you. Don't worry about it so much."

"Don't you worry if everyone likes you?"

"Not really, Jon."

"Really?"

"Yeah. Everyone usually does." I laughed as I gave him a rambunctious grin and took a sip of my beer. "Jon, I've had the same friends since I was old enough to be able to leave my house and venture out on my own. It's been me, Tierrah, and Regie since I can remember. Everyone else who I consider close like Gio, Tabitha, Danielle, Sarah, and whoever, are my girls for life. I'm sure I'll meet more people. I'm only twenty-three. However, my girls? I know I'll have them for life. I don't worry much about if the next person will like me or not. Treasure the connections you already have. Embrace new ones as they come, but don't worry about them. Be you. The people who are worth it will embrace you back. The ones who don't, won't."

"Don't, won't?"

"Jon, I'm drunk. You're perfect. Just be yourself. Everyone who knows you will love you. I love you. Kiss me."

"Here?"

"Yes."

"Seriously?" Tierrah walked between us. "I love you? Kiss me? What the hell is that?" She laughed. "Let's go."

Jon was embarrassed. I could see it in his face.

"I'm going to get the car going," he said, walking through the living room and then the front door.

"Okay. I've got to pee and see if I'm going to throw up or not," I sighed as I headed towards the bathroom.

...

I've always had horrible anxiety and then when I turned about eighteen and started occasionally smoking and drinking it intensified. I quickly learned that it was pointless to not attempt to throw up before I started drinking or before I went out because what would happen was I would have a few drinks and quickly vomit my buzz away.

There for a while in my early twenties it happened often. My body would get anxious nervous before it was time to head out and I would become nauseous. Before too long I realized if I would just go bend over in front of the toilet it would be a quick and easy process. My friends were used to it by the time I was twenty-one. It was normal. It's calmed down since then. Thank goodness. However, it still happens at times.

...

I stood above the toilet. Nothing. *Great.* I washed my hands and met Tierrah in the hallway.

"You're a mess," she laughed.

"I can't help it! My anxiety."

"I'm talking about him."

"Oh. Yeah. I know."

"As long as you know."

I went and told Brooke and Ken goodbye and found Tierrah waiting for me on the front porch.

"Let me sit in the front," she said as we walked towards the car.

"No way!"

"Why? You going to give him head on the way?"

"Seriously? You're gross, but thanks."

"If you weren't so tall I'd make you ride in the back. I don't care if he's your boyfriend or not."

"He isn't my boyfriend."

"Jasmine. He's your boyfriend. You say I love you and you're kissing him and sleeping with him and you're with him every day and night."

I smiled. "Just friends."

"Just friends my ass."

"You want me to just friends your ass?"

"You're an idiot, Jasmine."

"Tierrah?" I put my hand on the passenger door so she couldn't open it.

"What?"

"Do you or do you not want me to just friends your ass?"

She almost hit me with the car door as she opened it.

"I'm getting in the back, Jasmine."

"Wait."

"Jasmine, stop."

"Seriously, though. I'm being serious."

"What?!"

"Do you want me to just friends your ass?"

"You're the stupidest person I know," she laughed as she climbed in the back.

I plopped down next to Jon harder than I intended to.

"You good?"

"Yeah, Tierrah is just being inappropriate."

Tierrah reached up and shook my shoulder with her hand.

"I like the way you make her laugh," Jon said to Tierrah.

"You like the way I make her laugh? What kind of corny shit is that?"

Jon laughed. "I'm serious! You make her so happy."

"Jon. Drive," she said touching his shoulder. "And if it means anything, I like the way you make her laugh."

"I'm too drunk for this," I interrupted.

15

By the time we got to Magoos I was taking deep breaths to try and contain myself. I was more drunk than I thought. I took Jon's hand and led him inside.

"Jasmine!" Gio galloped my direction. "And Jon! Perfect!"

Jon smiled.

"See? Everyone." I winked at him. "I'm going to look in the mirror. Have fun."

I walked with Gio and Tierrah to the restroom to open up a few beers from my purse.

"Girl, look at you holding his hand," Gio said as she opened a beer and tossed the cap in the trash.

"Best friends." I smiled.

"Shit." Tierrah laughed.

"There's an after party tonight that Hillary is already at. You guys have to come!" Gio insisted.

"Yes, it's been a while," Tierrah said, accepting the invite.

We found Jon by the bar.

"I was asked three times if we were together," he said grabbing my arm.

"What? No."

"Yes."

"Well?"

"I said just friends." He shrugged.

"I bet they are just interested in you, Jon. You're hot."

"Probably not." He shrugged again.

"Whatever. But not tonight! Tonight you're mine!"

"Why are they asking, though?"

"We came in holding hands, Jon."

"So?"

"So? I'm never with a guy, Jon. They're either curious or interested in you."

"Probably just curious." He shrugged again.

"Jon, you're tall and hot and perfect." I kissed him. "Now they're really going to be curious."

He laughed. "You're crazy tonight."

"Let's just have fun." I grabbed his hand. "I've wanted you all day."

"What does that even mean?" He squeezed my hand.

"Come with me and I'll show you."

"What?"

I pulled him behind me and headed towards the restroom.

"Jasmine."

"Jon."

I led him to the door marked women's.

"Come in with me."

"Seriously?"

"Yes."

Before he could answer I started kissing him and pulled him in through the door by the bottom of his shirt to follow me.

"Excuse me," a girl laughed as she walked by and out of the restroom.

Jon pulled his lips from mine and gave her a quick "sorry.".

I pulled his lips back to mine and tried to back into a stall.

"I think we've got to pull it open," he said as he decided to take over.

He turned me around and pushed me against the wall away from the stall as he grabbed the top of the door to pull it open.

"I'm in here," came a voice.

We both started laughing as he opened the stall door next to it and backed inside smiling. I stood and smiled at him. He looked gorgeous. His hair messed up from me, his big dark eyes, and his hands in his pockets. I looked to the right as another girl walked in. I smiled and she smiled back. Before I could look back at Jon his arms exited the stall and pulled me in.

"Holy shit!" I heard the girl say.

I locked the door behind me and kissed Jon harder than we had ever kissed. After what seemed like the longest three minutes of romantic drawn out intense kissing with the toilets flushing, girls giggling, and knocks on the door in the background, we exited the bathroom hand in hand.

"Seriously?" Tierrah met us outside of the door.

"Let's dance." I pulled Jon to the dance floor. We danced two entire songs before the Cha Cha song came on.

"Let's take a break," he suggested.

"I don't want to stop," I blurted.

"You hate this song," he reminded me.

"Fine."

As I was walking with him off of the dance floor Tierrah grabbed my arm and pulled me back. I looked at Jon as she pulled me away.

"Go," he mouthed with a big smile.

16

I was expecting him to get lost in the crowd, but he stood there and watched me cha cha with a grin from ear to ear. I tried to move my hips as sexy as possible. I hate that song. I hate dancing to it more than I hate hearing it.

I stumbled a few times and he held out his hands from fifteen feet away as if he'd be able to catch me if I was to topple over.

I don't know if it was the alcohol, my semi-blurred vision, or Beyoncé in the background, but next thing I knew I was in a movie. I swear. Everyone was in slow motion, Jon was still standing there watching me, Beyoncé's voice and Tierrah's laugh filled the air, and I was dancing like Cierra. So I thought.

"Jasmine?"

I blinked and Jon was standing directly in front of me.

"You okay?"

"Yeah."

"You're just standing here."

"Huh? Yeah."

He took my hand. "Let's go sit down."

"Okay." I followed him to a nearby table and watched as Tierrah and Gio laughed and danced for a few more songs.

Jon placed his hand on top of mine. "You sure you're up for an after party?"

"Yeah."

"You look really pretty tonight."

I stared at him and we both laughed. He knew how much I hated compliments. We talked for the remaining hour or so while I drank water. I got up to dance a few times and Jon joined me a couple of those times.

"I think we are going to head to that party," Gio said as she walked over.

I could have closed my eyes and fallen asleep right then and there if I wanted. I was exhausted. I laid my head down on the table and closed my eyes while lifting my hand.

"Let's go."

"I'll carry you," Jon offered.

"Carry me!" Gio laughed.

"You better carry her." I motioned with my arms for her to hop on his back.

He gave her a piggy back ride through the lobby and out of the door to his car.

"You're the best, Jon!" she thanked him at his car. "You're driving, too?" She jumped up and down.

He stared at her.

"Get in, Gio." Tierrah opened the passenger door.

Gio started to get in the front.

"The back, Gio." Tierrah stopped her from completely getting in. Tierrah followed her into the back.

"Where to?" Jon asked after I was settled and closed the door. I looked at Gio.

"Girl, I don't know!"

"Call Hillary, Gio," Tierrah sighed.

I turned around, opened a beer, and handed one back to Tierrah.

"I want one!" Gio begged.

"Sorry, only one left."

"Boo!"

I called Hillary and put her on speaker so that Jon could note the directions.

He was quiet on the drive. Gio was on her phone drowning out the radio with laughter. I couldn't see Tierrah behind me, but I assume she was lost in text and drinking her beer.

I watched out the window as we passed buildings and eventually houses. I thought about JJ. I tried not to but that's the only place my brain would go. If he was here I'd either be at his house or crying over something or someone that he did. But, maybe not? Maybe we would be headed to a party after the bar with my friends. *There's no way. My friends hated him and he hated my friends.*

I looked at Jon. He kept his eyes on the road.

My thoughts returned to JJ. I wondered what he was doing at that moment. Was he thinking about me? Surely he was asleep.

"You okay?" Jon put his hand on my knee and squeezed.

"Stooooop. I hate that."

"Stoooooop," he mocked back.

We pulled up to a house that had all of its lights on.

"This is it I think," said Jon as he put the car in park.

Right as I was about to have Gio call Hillary I saw Hillary walk from the front door on her phone.

"You're here!" Her face lit up as she saw me open the door.

She said something and hung up her phone. She skipped over and hugged me tightly and kissed my cheek as I got out of the car.

"Soul sister! Come in," she insisted, pulling me by my hand.

"Everyone polite?" I asked as I climbed the hill to get to the porch.

"Of course, of course! Tierrah! Giovanna! Jon! Hello!" She lead the way and we followed her inside.

"She knows me?" Jon nudged my shoulder.

"I mean, I suppose! Everyone knows I've been hanging out with a Jon and it's obvious you're him. I told her you were coming."

He smiled and grabbed my hand. We entered an empty living room with a coffee table that had seven bottles of different types of alcohol, a bucket of ice, a few random juices, and some yellow solo cups.

"Help yourself!" Hillary offered.

Hillary and Gio disappeared down the hall.

Jon immediately grabbed two cups, did some mixing, and handed me and Tierrah each a cup.

"I like him!" Tierrah said as she patted my shoulder.

"I knew you would," I said, smiling at Jon.

17

We joined the party down the hall. The house had a couple of living areas as well as a back den. There was dancing, laughing, singing, and the entire time there was Jon. It felt good having him smile at me while we danced and having him laugh with me. He never cared how loud I laughed. He cheered me on while I joined drunk choruses of the most ridiculous old school rap songs.

...

I've never felt how Jon made me feel. I've had prior relationships, great ones in fact, but I was a teenager then. It was different. Now was different. And yes, there was JJ, but every bit of that was toxic. All Jon had to do was look at me and my insides would dance.

...

I was mumbling some rap song with Tierrah very aware of my words slurring when I felt Jon's hands on my hips from behind. He turned me around and started kissing me. Everyone started cooing and clapping as he pulled me towards him. He walked backwards while we continued to kiss.

"I need to pee." I managed to get out between breaths.

I asked the owner of the house where the restroom was and had to have her repeat it to me.

"I got it," Jon said as he took my hand and led the way.

We got to the bathroom and I quickly went in and closed the door behind me before he could enter. I opened the door back up and kissed him before I reclosed it and did my business. As I washed my hands I stared at my reflection wondering when I would next sleep again. I felt pretty. I wasn't sure if it was the alcohol or Jon or my eyeliner that was still in perfect unsmeared condition. I felt pretty and I knew what I wanted. Jon.

I opened up the door and he hadn't moved. I paused and stood in front of him for a good ten seconds without saying anything. His face stayed frozen. I grabbed him by his shirt and pulled him into the bathroom. He almost lost his balance.

"Jasmine."

"Just kiss me."

"What's with you tonight?"

"Kiss me, Jon."

He grabbed me by the chin and started kissing me. Before I knew it I was leaning backwards over the sink and he had my hands above my head against the mirror.

"Jon."

"You said you wanted me, right?"

"Yes."

"Well."

I pulled my hands from his and used them to put myself on the sink. His hands were in my hair and as I wrapped my legs around him he started kissing me slowly, moving from my neck to my lips then to the other side of my neck and back to my lips. He started to raise my shirt.

"Jon!"

He knew how nervous I was to take my shirt off. Even back then before having children and at least fifty pounds thinner, I've always been nervous to allow someone to see me.

"Come on."

"Okay," I sighed.

He neatly folded my top and put it on the shelf and turned around to look at me. I couldn't look at him. I nervously hummed. I focused my attention on his mouth, but could feel eyes scoping every inch of the top half of my body.

"You're so perfect, Jasmine; I don't know why you have to be so nervous."

"I'm just waiting," I said, not sure what I meant.

"For this?" He cupped my breast and stared into my eyes.

"Just kiss me," I demanded. I was beginning to feel awkward.

"Want me to turn the lights off?" he offered.

"No! What if we broke something?"

"You're right."

I looked down at his hands still holding each of my breasts. I looked back at him and he was smiling. I rolled my eyes and pulled him closer with my legs. He began massaging my nipples with his thumbs and I lost it. I grabbed the back of his head with both of my hands and forced my lips on his. He reached for my pants and I felt him searching for the button.

"There's no button." I somehow allowed the words to escape from our locked lips.

He started to tug my pants down.

"We are not hooking up on these people's sink."

"Hold on to me," he said as he picked me up.

I wrapped my arms around his neck. He carried me and then stood me by the toilet.

"Here?" I asked.

"It's a clean bathroom."

He put the lid down and took his pants off, leaving his underwear on. I followed suit and kept mine on as well. He pulled me on top of him. I was a little shocked with the realization I was strattling him on a stranger's toilet. He was pulling me with his left hand closer and closer to him, forcing me to move my hips exactly how I imagined he wanted me to. His right hand was behind my neck, not allowing me to take my lips from his.

I pushed him away and walked backwards to the light switch. I slowly took my panties off. I flipped the switch downward and held my hands out in front of me to find my way back to him. The bathroom was big. He lit up his phone for me to follow the light to him.

I sat on top of him and grabbed both sides of his face and held it. He lifted me up and sat me down on top of him with all of him inside of me. I could barely breathe.

After we were finished I quickly put my clothes back on.

"Red underwear and black bra, huh?" Jon laughed as I struggled with my bra strap.

"Shut up," I said as I finally succeeded in buckling it.

I turned around and slipped my shirt on. I went to the mirror to fix my hair.

"You look great," he said while slipping on his shoes.

"Shut up," I said again.

He laughed.

"I'm going first," I said as I grabbed my phone.

"Really?"

"Yes!" I reached for the door knob and turned it. "Seriously?" I gasped.

"What?" he asked. I turned the knob and it came right open.

"It was unlocked the entire time!"

He laughed again.

"Shut up!" I said as I walked out and closed the door behind me.

It took me a few minutes to find Tierrah.

"Gio is going to stay with Hillary," Tierrah

said as she chugged a water bottle of water on the couch.

"You ready?" I asked.

"Yes, please. Where's Jon?"

I shrugged. "I don't know. He's probably in the bathroom I think."

"I can't believe you two aren't together," she said as he walked into the room.

"Where have you been?" Tierrah asked.

"The restroom." Jon laughed.

We left.

The days played out on repeat. We'd go out, hang out, work, and repeat.

Jon had been missing his sister, Lily. He kept making plans to surprise her with a vacation. He wanted to go to either Florida or California. He could never make up his mind.

I rarely kept in contact with JJ. I kept in contact with his mother, but other than that, I barely wrote.

I had encouraged Jon to talk to other girls, but to not let me know about it. He'd bring girls up at times but would become bored with the topic when I acted like I didn't care. It bothered me at times, but at the end of most days he was with me, so it was always easy for me to shrug off.

I came home one day and he was sleeping on my couch. I can't remember if I was about to start my period or if I was just in a bad mood, but I was completely annoyed. I rolled my eyes as I stomped past and fell on my bed for a nap. I woke up a few hours later to Jon playing with my hair.

"What are you doing here?" I asked.

"Damn. Really?"

"Sorry, I don't know what's wrong."

"Period?" He knew me too well.

"Probably." I didn't feel annoyed anymore.

"Want some ice cream? Pickles or something?"

I laughed. "Jon, you're crazy. I think that's for pregnant women."

"Emotionally unstable. Pregnant. Tomato, tomoto."

I kissed him.

"Let's go to the store. I need some socks," he said tapping his knees.

"Carry me?" I held my arms to him.

He took the blanket off of me. "Jasmine! You're why I need socks!"

I looked at my feet and wiggled my toes that were hidden in a pair of his socks.

"They're so comfy! And they match. This is my favorite pair. I only have this pair, I swear!"

"Fine, you can keep them but you have to keep them forever."

"You're so corny. Let's go. Come on, Madalynn!" I loved how he was okay with me bringing her everywhere.

We got to Walmart and got the essentials; socks, ramen noodles, water, and chocolate milk.

As we were checking out Jon asked, "Did you see those cats outside?"

"The kittens?"

"Yes. Let's get one."

"Seriously, Jon?"

"Jasmine, you said so yourself that Madalynn needs company while you're gone at work."

"Jon."

"Jasmine."

"Jon!"

"Jasmine!"

He paid the cashier and took my hand. We walked to my car and he opened the door and got in the driver seat.

"Okay?" I said as I walked to the passenger side.

I tossed him the keys. Madalynn hopped in my lap.

"You want a baby?" Jon asked Madalynn while petting the top of her head.

"Jon, no!"

He pulled the car out and drove to where a mother and who I assumed to be her daughter were sitting with two huge boxes. He opened the door and called Madalynn out.

This is really about to happen, I thought as I opened my door to join them.

The meows coming from the two boxes of kittens were equally adorable as they were annoying. Jon and I approached the boxes as Madalynn found a spot nearby to relieve herself. One box had four kittens and the other only had one.

"Why is this one alone?" Jon asked.

"She is the only female left," the woman said as she picked her up and handed her to Jon.

He called Madalynn over and bent down so Madalynn could examine her. "Meet your new sister, Madalynn," he said while looking up at me. "We will take her," he said to the woman as he stood up.

"God bless," she replied and turned to walk away.

The little girl grabbed my hand and handed me a flower and motioned me down to her level. I got down on one knee.

She whispered in my ear, "She's my favorite."

"I'll take really good care of her, I promise." I touched her nose as I stood up.

I turned to catch up with Jon and the little girl hugged me from behind. I picked her up and carried her to the box of male kittens. I sat her down and picked up a kitten that looked similar to the kitten Jon had picked out.

"Here. Take him. It is your favorite kitten's twin brother."

She held the kitten to her face.

"Bless your kind soul," her mother said to me, "You're an angel."

I smiled and turned to walk away.

"Wait!" The little girl shouted.

"Yes, sweet?"

"What is your kitten's name?"

"Her name?" I paused. "Latika. Her name is Latika."

"Latika," she repeated.

"Yes. Latika. Have a fun day with your mother, okay?"

"Okay, ma'am," she said as she held the kitten to her face.

I heard her say Latika again as I was walking off.

Jon was in the front seat holding both Latika and Madalynn.

"Kids love you," he said as I put my seat belt on.

"Mhmm," I agreed as I started the car.

He put Latika on my lap. Madalynn sat up and perked her ears. My lap was her spot.

"Get in back," I motioned to her. She immediately hopped in back and jumped to her spot in the back window.

I held Latika up with one hand. She was black with random orange and white markings. I would have never had picked her and could see why she was the last female left.

"Well, hello Miss Latika," I said as I rubbed her tiny body on my face. "Suppose we ought to get you some food and a place to poop."

"Latika?" Jon asked.

"Latika." I confirmed.

"Beautiful."

"It's from my favorite movie."

"Of course it is."

Latika was a good cat and Madalynn loved her. I particularly was amused with how she would watch me shower.

Jon would clean her litter box when he came over and would buy her food even though I insisted I would handle it.

I was showering one night and here she came making herself comfortable on the ledge of the tub.

"Well, hello, Miss. Where is your sister?"

She meowed and looked back over her shoulder.

Really, God? I thought to myself. I continued with my shower when she started meowing.

"What's wrong?"

She jumped on the sink and circled Jon's face wash and nudged it with her nose into the sink.

"I miss him, too girl."

She hopped off the sink and left me alone.

When I got out of the shower I picked Jon's wash out of the sink and realized it was empty. I almost threw it away but instead I put it in a basket beneath the sink. It wasn't mine to throw away. I sent Jon a text to let him know he was out of face wash. I still have the empty bottle.

It had been a while since I had been home alone, so I decided to take a nap in my towel. I woke up three hours later and opened my eyes to Madalynn and Latika curled up next to my naked body.

19

On Mother's Day Jon was super excited. He loved his mother. I was excited to spend the day with him and see what would come of that day's adventure.

Alex and Jon showed up at my apartment at about noon. They had agreed to go by my mother's house with me.

Something about that Mother's Day had me thinking about Cindy, my old babysitter who had passed away some years before. Jon could tell I had something on my mind. He always knew.

"What's up, Jas? Your mood is off."

"Would you mind riding with me to my babysitter's grave? She was like a mother to me and-"

He put his hand on mine. "You don't have to explain, Jasmine. Let's go now so we can fit all three moms in."

I jumped on him and knocked him back on my couch.

"What are you doing?"

"I love you so much, Jon. I'm serious. You're the best person I've ever met."

"It's no big deal, Jas."

"What's up with you calling me Jas?"

He smiled. "Laziness I guess."

"Nerd. Let's go."

We drove to the graveyard where Cindy is buried. There were already fresh flowers on her grave. That made me smile. Jon grabbed my hand as we stood there.

"You will have to tell me all about her someday."

"I will. Let's go. Thank you, guys. Thanks, Jon."

"What's up with you calling me Jon and not Jonathaon?"

"Laziness I guess."

We left and went straight to my mother's house. Her flowers were in full bloom as they were every year for Mother's Day, so I had him and Alex each hold one and stand at the door. I rang the doorbell and hid. My mother came to the door and started laughing as the boys stood there smiling.

I came around the corner singing.

"Mommaaaaaa. Mommaaaaa, you knoooow I love youuuuu."

The guys handed her her flowers and I handed her her gift. She had tears in her eyes. I wasn't sure if it was from laughing or just from the emotional mess of genes she had passed on to me.

"Thanks, baby." She hugged me and held her arms out to the guys as well. "You boys come here, too!"

I was in a group hug with my mother and two guys. This never happened before.

We didn't stay long because we had to meet with Nate and Jon's mother at Olive Garden.

On the way to eat Alex played old school rap. It was a quiet drive minus the occasional rap outbursts we'd each have. I was nervous to meet Jon's mom. He was excited.

When we arrived I hesitated to get out of the car. After I finally got out Jon took my hand.

"No way, Jon."

"What?"

"I'm not walking in here holding your hand. Oh, hello! Nice to meet you. I'm not Jon's girlfriend but we're in love and best friends but can't be together and-"

"Okay. Shut up." He interrupted.

"You two are too much sometimes," Alex said as he opened the door for us to enter.

Jon's mother was already waiting on us with Nate. She stood up and hugged Jon as we made it to the table. He picked her up a few inches off of the ground.

"Dammit, Jon, put me down," she laughed.

She was smiling ear to ear. She opened up her arms to Alex and then to me.

"You must be Jasmine. You're beautiful!" she said as she hugged me.

"Thank you so much. It's so nice to meet you. Happy Mother's Day."

We sat and had wine and a delightful dinner. We laughed and chatted the entire time. I felt like I had always known his mother. He was a wonderful reflection of her. She was kind and open and easy to converse with.

Dinner lasted a little over two hours due to our food taking forever. We barely noticed, though. It was an incredible time.

After we were finished we all hugged and said our goodbyes. Jon's mother thanked us and said she couldn't wait to see us again and instructed us to care for her son. He walked her to her car as Alex and I walked to the Mustang.

We dropped Alex off on the way back to our apartments. Jon stopped at a convenient store to get gas.

"Need anything?"

"No, thank you, Jon. I just need a nap."

When he returned to the car he handed me a flower from the flower pot that was next to the convenient store's entrance.

"Happy Mother's Day, Jasmine. From Madalynn and Latika to the best mother ever."

We both looked at it and then at each other and laughed.

"Thank you, Jon. And thank you to my beautiful daughters."

20

That night I told Jon we needed to get to the liquor store before it got too late to purchase alcohol.

"You're drinking tonight? On Mother's Day? It's Sunday, Jas, and you have both jobs to work tomorrow," he said as he looked in his wallet, I assume to see how much cash he had.

"Yes. My brother's birthday is in a few days, so I think I'm going to have people over to celebrate. I'm due to have a party at my place," I said with a big grin, rubbing my hands together. "I'm just going to have close friends and family. You down?"

"It's your place so it doesn't matter if I'm down or not. But yes, I'm down."

"Good. I work doubles all week so I'd rather go now and get it over with. I need to catch up on sleep."

We got to the store. As I grabbed my wallet to go in, Jon handed me a twenty.

"What's this for?" I asked. "You want to get your stuff now?"

"Get whatever Jeremiah's favorite drink is," he said with a smile, "and use my money so it's one hundred percent from me."

"You're sweet. Okay." I went in and got the supplies I needed as well as a gift for Jeremiah to be specifically from Jon.

...

That week went by in a flash. Jon packed a bag and ended up staying with me for the entire week. I didn't mind. I enjoyed not being alone even though when I was home I was only awake long enough to shower and go to bed.

That Thursday I had fallen asleep on the couch. I thought I had imagined my phone ringing three times in a row but was woken up to Jon holding it in my face.

"Your phone is blowing up. I didn't mean to look, but Janelle has been calling you and I think she sent a few texts."

"Okay."

I took the phone. As soon as I was about to reply and let her know I had been sleeping, there was a knock at the door.

"Come in!" I shouted.

Jon opened the door.

"Well hello, cutie. Who are you?" Janelle said as she entered.

Jon smiled. "I'm Jon."

"Jazzy. I've been wanting to come see the crib and Ron is out so I wanted to stop by. I was going over to see my cousin and was hoping you'd be home." She came and sat down next to me.

"Sorry I didn't answer, I've worked doubles all week."

"Girl, I don't know how you do it, but you do it. If anyone could, it'd be you."

"It's all about that cash money," I laughed.

"Who you telling? So, who is this cutie? Jon?" She looked towards the kitchen.

We couldn't see Jon because he was around the corner in the fridge or something.

"It's Jon, who I've been talking about. He is cute though, you're right."

We both laughed.

Jon came back in the living room and sat and talked with Janelle.

"You going to be here a while?" I asked Janelle.

"As long as you don't kick me out."

She and Jon both laughed.

"Okay," I said, "I'm going to take a quick shower. I'll be right back."

I left them alone in the living room and took a quick shower with Latika. After I was finished they were both laughing loudly. I threw some clothes on and joined them.

"Not hair night?" Janelle asked when I joined them on the couch. "Does he know about our wonderful African American heritage and the time it takes us to tame our fros?"

"Yes, Janelle. He knows. And nope, not hair night for me."

She turned to Jon, "Well, what do you think about all Jazzy has to do for her hair to look how it does? Have you seen the process?"

"Yeah. I've seen her hair curly, wet, and I've seen her straighten it and put a relaxer on it as well. She has beautiful hair."

"So, when are you two getting married?" she asked with a big smile. "Jasmine. I love this dude. He's genuine and real and he loves the Lord."

"Loves the Lord?" I was confused how she got that out of him saying he's seen me do my hair.

"We had ourselves a heart to heart while you were showering."

Jon and I looked at each other. He was smiling. He shrugged.

Janelle was looking at us both going back and forth with her eyes.

"You two are just too cute," Janelle said, "It looks like you're reading each other's minds. Really Jazz. I like him."

"She doesn't love me enough," he laughed.

"Oh, so you're down and ready to love this woman?" She clapped her hands. "Miss. Jasmine is the whole package. I'm sure you know that already."

"Janelle. I'm tired. I've got to get some sleep before I'm back on the grind in the morning."

"So, you're kicking me out, Jazzy? I see how it is."

"Janelle."

"You know I'm kidding." She looked at Jon. "Jon? It was awesome to meet you my dude! Jazz is going to have to bring you over to my place soon. You two are going to have to come out to Ron's birthday party at the casino next month!"

"Most definitely," Jon agreed. "We will be there for sure!"

"This is the man right here! I'll see you soon, sister." She hugged me and then hugged Jon. After she left I looked at Jon.

"I've got to sleep. You sleeping here?"

"Yeah. And I want to go to the casino with her next month. Can we?"

"Of course. However, you stink. You going to shower?"

"Yes. I need you to do me a favor, though."

"Whaaaaat?" I slouched over and walked to my bedroom and fell on my bed.

"Sleep naked."

"Jon."

"Please?"

"Okay."

21

Jeremiah's birthday had been Wednesday, so I planned to have everyone over that Saturday. As much as I wanted to celebrate on Friday so I could spend the weekend recovering from all the doubles followed by a party, I couldn't.

I came home Friday and crashed hard. Jon ended up working later than me. I got to my place and fell asleep still wearing my work clothes before I could message him.

I woke up in the middle of the night. Jon had only called twice, but text a few times letting me know he couldn't get in and was going to go out with his bro. Something like that. I was too out of it. That was probably the longest week of my life. However, I had quite the wad of cash from Savannah's as well as a full forty hours for the week from the preschool. I was happy.

...

Jon ended up coming over around noon the next day already smelling good and ready for that evening's festivities.

"You look so good," I said.

He started heating up left over pizza that he brought with him.

"I'm excited for tonight," he said. "Which of your brothers are coming over?"

"Just Jason and Jeremiah that I know of. Tierrah is coming and she's bringing her step brother. It's going to be a random night. I'm going to set up beer pong, though, and get some food. I wish I wasn't so tired."

"You sleep and I will get everything set up," he said as he handed me some pizza and garlic sauce. "Eat and then I'll wake you up in a couple of hours."

"Really?"

I knew he was serious but didn't want to come off as too eager or needy. I took a bite of my pizza and kissed his cheek.

"Yes. Now hurry and eat."

"You're the best."

"I know. If only you'd realize that."

"I do."

"Then let me put you to bed."

"That is so lame sounding. But, okay."

Afterwards I slept until four.

When I woke up I was still exhausted. That week kicked my ass. However, I had a lot of missed texts asking if the night was still a go.

As much as I wanted to cancel and sleep more, I didn't.

Jon had gone to the store while I was asleep and got some snack foods. I spent the next few hours cleaning and replying to everyone's text. I also let all of my neighbors in the building know I was planning to have a party and pre-apologized for any loud noise.

Everyone started to show up around nine. I say everyone, but there were no more than ten that showed up, which was perfect because my apartment wasn't very big.

We all cheered for Jeremiah as he arrived. Jon was so excited to give him his gift.

"Hey man, thanks!" Jeremiah said as Jon handed him his drinks.

The party was a success. I somehow managed to make the beer pong table fit in my kitchen perfectly. The music was good and everyone was laughing and enjoying themselves. Tierrah brought her stepbrother and everyone drew a bit in my notebook I had on the table.

As much fun as everyone was having, I sat back on the couch and did most of my visiting from there. I couldn't overcome my exhaustion. Jon came and sat with me at the end of the night during the last beer pong tournament between my brother and Tierrah. My friend, Sarah, sat on the other side of me.

"Say cheese!" she said. I turned and heard the click from the camera of her phone.

It was about three in the morning when everyone left. Jon and Sarah stayed behind to help me clean up.

"I had a blast!" Jon said as he helped me wipe up the kitchen floor. "Your brothers really seemed to like me and that one dude with the long braids was chill!"

"Of course." I smiled.

"You okay?" Sarah asked.

"I'm so tired, girl. I think I'm going to go to bed. I will finish this tomorrow."

"Do you mind if I sleep on your couch?" Sarah asked as she emptied two drinks into the sink.

"My casa is your casa, Sarah. Goodnight."

"I'll be right there, babe." Jon said as I headed down the hallway. "I'm going to take the trash out."

I woke up alone the next afternoon at one o' clock to a spotless apartment.

22

That next week at Alex's, Jon and Alex were discussing Memorial Day weekend plans. They wanted to go to the lake. I wanted to go to the river.

"Let's just do both," Jon said smiling at me and juggling three small balls. "I can get someone to work for me and we will make it happen."

"No one will work for you, Jon," Alex chimed in.

"Bet," Jon answered. He picked up his phone and started to message someone.

"How will we do both?" I asked. "And Tierrah said she is down to come too no matter what we do. We just have to have a plan first. Trust me; the river is the place to be. Every single person I have talked to is going to be there and neither of you have ever been before."

Jon sat his phone down. "Momma D is going to work for me."

"Wow," Alex said as he stood up and headed to the kitchen to make something to eat.

"Let's go to the lake on Sunday and head back Monday afternoon to the river," Jon said, tapping his fingers on the table. "That's when the river party is, right? Monday?"

"Yes." I raised and lowered my eyebrows. "Yesssssss. Alex? Yes?"

"Yes," Alex said looking up smiling.

"Plans are made then," Jon said as he tossed a ball to me. "Let Tierrah know. Ask her if we can take her car since it has the most space."

Tierrah agreed to the plans and said Ken would be joining us for the river on Monday. Everyone was talking about the river. I had been a few times the previous summer, but had been told to never return due to a fight that broke out one night. It was self-defense. But oh well. It had been a year. Surely the owner wouldn't remember me.

...

That Friday I had to work both jobs and Jon was scheduled to work a double at the restaurant. I left my phone at home by accident, so when I got home to get ready to head to Savannah's I had twelve missed texts. I smiled and grabbed Madalynn to head outside.

As Madalynn and I were walking behind our building I began to read my phone. None of the messages were from Jon. *Oh.* I immediately started missing him. He had told me he had been planning to hang out with a girl he knew. My mind went to him and her. *I bet he messaged her. If he can message her, he can message me.*

Stop it, Jasmine.

After Madalynn finished up, I emptied Latika's box to toss it in the dumpster on my way out. I told the girls goodbye and headed downstairs. As I tossed the bag into the dumpster my phone went off.

Jon: Hey. See you soon?
Me: Sure.
Jon: Why sure?
Me: It means yes.
Jon: It means something is wrong. What's wrong?
Me: Nothing.
Jon: I know what's wrong.
Me: Of course you do.

Jon: I've been really busy today. I miss you too. See you.

I got to Savannah's and the place was slammed. I immediately started stocking both wait stations and taking tables. Jon was stationed in the back so we didn't talk much. No one talked much. It was the busiest night I had ever had there.

"Let's go, let's go!" Travis called from the back. "Everyone is in town, get this food out and keep them happy!"

His brother started mouthing him. I hoped to see a fight between them. When they fought it was always amusing. Their love-hate relationship was real. You could tell Travis was upset at whatever his brother said because he slammed a plate down.

"You two!" Vince yelled, "Stop the shit!"

The night ended late and everyone had made a large chunk of cash. Cleaning up was fun. I was over being butt hurt about not hearing from Jon that day. He won me over by standing in my freshly mopped area doing a dance that involved him sliding all over the floor.

I heard loud music playing in the kitchen. I went to see what was going on. All of the kitchen crew were having a c walking dance-off. Everyone was laughing and having a great time.

"This is the best night of work," Jon said laughing. "I'm so happy to work here and I made over two hundred today."

"That's awesome!" I said, "Cash money. Let's get out of here." I made sure I saved the video of Jon dancing and the guys battling.

As we walked to our cars I stopped and looked at Jon. "Did you message that girl? The one you had been talking about? Did you message her today?"

"Really?"

"Yes."

"Well, yes."

"Oh."

"She messaged me. You didn't message me. I was swamped today."

"I didn't have my phone."

"Are you jealous?" He smiled.

"Yes."

"You still love me?"

"Sure."

"Want me to not message her?"

"No. I want you to invite her to the lake with us."

"Really?"

"Yes. But I've gotta go. I want to go right to sleep so I can get my apartment spotless and laundry done before we leave Sunday."

I got in my car and shut the door before he could say anything. He stood at his car and watched me as I drove away.

I was throwing a fit. Of course I didn't want her to go. There I was ruining a perfect night for myself. *What do they talk about? Does she make him smile like I do? I'm sure she does. She definitely does.*

Stop it, Jasmine.

I didn't message Jon at all for the remainder of the night. He didn't message me either. I put my phone on silent. I went to sleep telling myself if he were to text I wouldn't wake up to read it.

I woke up every hour that night and checked my phone. Nothing. I was driving myself crazy.

This is what you wanted.

23

The next day I worked the morning shift at Savannah's. I only had two tables in two hours. Travis said I could go home if I wanted.

"This is shit," he said looking at his phone.

"Everyone is gone today or headed to the lake," I said. "Yesterday was great." I gave him a quick shoulder massage. "You should come with me and the guys to the lake."

"I'll pass. Some of us have work to do."

"Tierrah is going. Come on." I squeezed his shoulders a bit harder.

"Oh, okay. I'll come then."

"Really?"

"No."

"Asshole."

"You know you love me. Now get out of here. Tell Jon not to come in until five."

"Why me?" I huffed.

"He's your husband. Boyfriend. Butt buddy. Whatever. Just tell him."

"You tell him. I've gotta get packed for my weekend."

"Jasmine. Message Jon and tell him to be here at five. Don't act like you aren't going to see him before then. It's one o' clock."

"Sir, yes, sir." I smiled. "And you're right. I do love you."

"Yeah, yeah. Have fun this weekend. And be safe."

"Always."

I took my twelve dollars and headed home.

...

It was the perfect May weather. Not too hot, not too cold. After Madalynn did her business we went to the swings diagonal from my building and I swayed back and forth as she sun bathed not too far from my feet. I got my phone out.

Me: Travis said not to come in until 5.
Jon: Are we dead?
Me: I left at 1
Jon: …..
Me: ?

I sat there another few minutes and felt myself starting to doze off.

The swings were my second favorite part of my apartment complex. My first favorite was the area Jon and I discovered that when the wind was blowing just right during a storm it felt like a vacuum vortex. *Jon, Jon, Jon, Jon, Jon.*

"Jon!" I screamed as he came up behind me and gave me a push.

I almost fell out of the swing. Madalynn stood up and greeted him with her tail going crazy.

"I miss you, Jasmine."

"Idiot. And we were together less than twenty-four hours ago."

"Things are weird." He joined me on the swings. "You're being weird and I'm not used to you being weird. Everything feels weird right now. Not just with you, but everything."

"You're weird."

"I'm serious, Jasmine. I feel so eager right now and I don't know what I'm eager for. You know how you have all of these feelings and thoughts and as you're thinking them they sound so intelligent and you need to get them out? But then you're like, who do I tell? What do I say?"

"Sort of."

"Sort of?"

"Actually, yes."

"Yes? See? What is it?"

"When I feel that way, I feel like it's God. I feel like it's Him talking to me trying to tell me something."

We sat in silence and swung for a few minutes without looking at each other.

"Look," I broke the silence, "in case it is, you know, God, you should focus. You've got to try to differentiate the difference between your own voice and His. I suggest talking back. Like right now." I continued, "You're telling me these feelings and out of everyone in your life for you to tell these feelings to, I'm telling you it's most likely Him. If I were you, I'd be taking that as His voice being spoken through me to let you know He wants you to hear Him."

He stopped swinging.

"Jasmine." He said as he stood up. "I just felt chills."

"See? God." I smiled. "You hungry?"

"Yeah, and so is Alex. Let's go eat. Let's take my car. I'll run and get it while you put the girl up. Kiss Latika for me."

I got up and headed towards my building. Madalynn started following Jon.

"Madalynn!" I yelled.

She turned around and began following me as if she were planning to come with me the whole time.

Jon turned around and started jogging backwards.

"I love you, Jasmine!" he yelled. "I love you, I love you, I love you!"

I felt myself blushing as I put my finger to my lips and turned to go up my stairs.

Jon, Jon, Jon, Jon.

24

Me: Did you take your sock back?
Jon: Sock?
Me: I only have one. Where's the other sock?
Jon: ?

    Jon came through the front door without knocking. I jumped a little.
    "What are you talking about? Did I take one sock?" he said with his face squinted.
    "I can only find one of your socks. They're my favorite and I want to wear my Converse. All my laundry is here, but that one sock is gone. It doesn't make sense."
    "You're losing your mind." He said opening my sock drawer.
    "See?" I pointed. "It's not there."
    "Wear sandals. Let's go. Alex is waiting and I've gotta work in two hours."
    "Fine," I huffed as I took the one sock off and tossed it in my sock drawer.
    Jon put the girls up for me and we headed to grab Alex.

"You all packed and ready?" I asked Alex as I climbed in the back to let him ride up front.

"I've been packed and ready," he said in his always serious tone.

"Of course." I laughed.

Jon looked back at me and smiled.

"Did you invite the girl?" I asked without thinking.

Alex looked at Jon and then turned and looked back at me and then back at Jon and then down at his phone. *Alex must know exactly what and who I'm talking about. Fucking bullshit.*

"Yeah," Jon answered after an awkward minute of silence.

Alex looked back at him and then back to his phone.

You're doing this to yourself.

We pulled up to the hidden Mexican restaurant on the square. It was hidden behind a Mexican store. I say hidden because unless you knew about it or could read Spanish, you'd never know it was there. It was also in the very back of the store. It was the second time the guys had brought me there. I always felt like we were going to some secret hideout in Mexico to eat. Jon always ordered for me. My favorite part was opening my old fashioned Cokes there. I saved the lids.

"We will leave at noon tomorrow," Alex said as he squeezed lime on his taco. "Are we still taking Tierrah's car?"

"Yes," I answered. "Is it just us four riding together?" I looked at Jon.

"Stop it, Jasmine." Jon rolled his eyes as he bit into his food. He knew exactly what I was doing.

After we finished up I stuck my Coke lid in my pocket and stretched as the guys thanked the cook for our meal.

Jon grabbed my hand as he walked past. He guided me through the hidden doors and through the store back to America.

We stopped by Alex's house and waited for him to run upstairs and grab his polo and apron for work.

Jon broke the silence. "I won't have her come if you don't want her to."

"Do you want her to?"

"You told me to invite her. You. So, why not?"

"I don't know what you want me to say, Jon. Have her come. I think it will be fun with more people."

"She may not even come. But, I did invite her. Only because that's what you told me to do."

Alex got back in the car. "You packed and ready to go?" he turned and asked as Jon pulled off.

"I'm packing tonight." I tried to sound like I wasn't about to cry.

The drive to my apartment was quiet. Jon blasted his favorite song at the time on repeat. He and Alex nodded and occasionally broke out in song. Alex reached over and turned it down. He looked back at me.

"You have a rap for this song?"

I laughed. "Not today."

"Come on, Jas. I know you have it in you."

We pulled up to my apartment.

"Next time," I said before I crawled out. "Bye, guys."

"See you in a bit," Alex said through his rolled down window.

I looked at Jon. He looked back at me. Then he drove off.

This is what you wanted.

25

The next morning Tierrah came to my apartment packed and ready to go. She laughed at my one small bag I had for myself.

"That's ridiculous," she said, lifting my bag.

"I only brought what I need! Which is nothing really."

"We are camping. Whatever you say." She tossed my bag onto the couch.

I only packed two changes of clothes and two swimsuits. I had my hair brush and a toothbrush and a bag with a couple rolls of toilet paper and a towel in it. I've never been big on packing. Easy peasy.

"You have the tent?" I asked as I wadded up my comforter to bring with us.

"Oh, shit! I forgot to tell you that Ken couldn't find it!"

"Tierrah!"

"Kidding. I have everything. Where are the guys?"

"Jon will be here soon. His mother is going to come by I believe. Then we will grab

Alex along the way. Do you want something to eat?"

"I already ate. I think I'm going to lay down and take a power rest before we leave. What are you going to make?"

"Scrambled eggs." I peeked around the corner to see her reaction.

"Your famous eggs with cheese? Okay, yes." She laughed as she stretched out on my couch.

Jon came over as I finished up with breakfast. I made us each a plate and had them join me in the kitchen to eat.

"Where are your bags?" Tierrah asked Jon.

"Right inside my front door," he answered. "I didn't want to drive or carry them over here."

I cleaned up breakfast and we lounged around on our phones. I heard a knock on the door.

"It's my mother," Jon said as he opened the door.

His mother came inside and gave him a hug and talked to him about being in town and being glad she got to come and visit him.

"How have you been, Jasmine?" she asked as she gave me a hug.

"All has been well! This is my friend, pretty much sister, Tierrah." I pointed at Tierrah who was still stretched out across my couch.

"It looks like you guys are ready," his mother said, looking around my apartment. "I want you all to be safe and not get too crazy."

"Of course, Mom." Jon kissed her forehead.

"I mean, I want you to have a good time. You know that." She smiled. "I'm going to get going. It was good to see everyone and meet you." She giggled and looked at Tierrah who was now asleep.

"Thank you for coming over," I said.

I opened the door while she hugged Jon.

"Of course, sweetie." She hugged me and walked out.

As the door was closing we made eye contact as she went down the stairs. It gave me the chills for some reason. I told Jon.

"You're weird," he said as he looked at his phone. "We should get going. Want to have a quickie?"

"You're ridiculous," I scolded. "Is that girl coming?"

"She said she was going to try, but I haven't heard from her. Want me to call her?"

"Get the hell out of my house." I pushed him backwards hard enough for him to take a step back.

"What? I'm serious. You really confuse me about what you want."

"I want to go. Let's go." I turned around and looked at Tierrah. "Tierrah, wake up. It's time."

"I wasn't asleep," she said as she raised up yawning.

We loaded up the car, went and grabbed Jon's things, then headed to Alex's.

...

"Let's get this show on the road!" Alex said as he got in the back with Jon after loading his stuff into the trunk.

I noticed Jon had on my wooden necklace.

"How long have you had that?" I reached back and tugged on it.

"You didn't even notice it was gone. Just let me keep it. You have two of them."

"You're a dirty thief!" I said as I crossed my arms.

"What's mine is yours, right? Come on." He turned around and the conversation was over.

It was a couple hours' drive to the lake if I remember right. Jon fell asleep for a little bit and Tierrah, Alex, and I rode in silence. About an hour into the drive we made the plan to pull over at a gas station to get some drinks and snacks.

I woke Jon up as Tierrah and Alex got out of the car to go inside.

"Babe. You need anything from here?"

He jolted up from his sleep.

"Whoa, are you okay?" I put my hand on his knee.

"Yeah." He yawned. "Did you just call me Blake?"

"Yes," I laughed, "Blake, do you need anything from the store?"

"Are you going to go in?" he asked with another yawn.

"No. I gave Tierrah money to grab me some stuff."

"I'm good. Can I ask you something?" he said, fixing his hair. "And you can't think I'm weird. I want an honest and straight answer."

"Okay," I nervously answered.

"When we hook up, how is it? Is it good? Is everything good? Every part of me good?"

"Really?" I never imagined that to be the question he'd be asking.

"I'm serious, yes. It's been on my mind and no one has ever really said anything and I know you'll be honest with me."

"Jon, you're like, the best at everything. Just trust me. Every part of you is perfect. Like, I swear."

"You don't have to say any of that to me. My feelings aren't going to get hurt. I just really want to know."

"And I'm being serious. It's seriously the best. The bessssst."

Tierrah got back in the car. "He's awake! You need anything? Because if you do, you'll need to call Alex." She laughed as she got situated in her seat and handed me my chips.

"I'm good, thank you." He laughed.

Alex got in the car a few minutes later and we took off. I turned around and looked at Jon.

"Every inch of you is perfect." I winked.

He smiled.

"You two are ridiculous." Alex glared at each of us as he opened his drink.

When we got to the lake I was surprised to see that even though there were vehicles and campers everywhere, I barely saw any people.

    We drove around for a few minutes before we found a small opening to park. We were perfect walking distance from the lake and we didn't have any neighboring campers too close for comfort.

    There was only one problem. No cell phone service. No matter where I went or walked to, I had zero bars. It was the same for everyone. The guys had reception bars that would appear and disappear. But other than that, nothing.

    We walked around to check everything out before we started to unpack. There was a long dock that led out to a row of parked boats if you went one way and to a restaurant on the lake if you went the other. There was a small store connected to it as well if you wanted to buy tackle or do whatever else lake people do.

    Tierrah beat me back to our camp site and turned her car on so that we could listen to music while we set up our tents. She blared her music loud enough for all to hear. I grabbed my phone and made a quick music video to capture the moment.

Jon danced over and wrapped his arms around me. "Kiss me?"

I smiled and looked around to see if anyone was watching before I kissed him. I wanted to ask him about the girl, but couldn't bring myself to do it.

"Come down to the water with me," he said as he took my hand.

"We've gotta help with the tents." I pulled away.

"Alex is a professional. He's got it."

We started to head towards the lake. I looked back and Tierrah had her hands up in the air. I waved. She flipped me off. Alex laughed.

"I really don't want to get my hair wet," I said as Jon and I started to enter the water.

"Of course you don't," Jon said lightly splashing me. "Want me to carry you?"

"I'm just not going to go out that far. But, yes I want you to carry me." I splashed him back.

"Let's kiss in the lake," Jon said as he slowly came towards me smiling. "Let's kiss all weekend."

"What about when your friend gets here?"

He stopped coming towards me and rolled his eyes. "Really?"

"Really."

"I have no service. I can't get a hold of her or anyone." He shrugged and turned around. "Are you going to be like this all weekend?"

"Maybe."

He turned around and splashed me.

"Jon!"

"I don't care. I'm taking you under."

I turned and tried to move quickly through the water and back to the shore. He chased after me. I made it to land and ran up the hill. He stayed behind and called Alex down to join him. I watched from our spot as he and Alex swam and talked about whatever.

Tierrah and I straightened up our tent and walked down to the shore to see what the guys wanted to do next.

"We're going to walk the land and try to get some service. Want to come?" Jon asked as he shook the water out of his hair.

"We are going to go explore, just us," Tierrah answered.

I had no idea of such a plan.

Jon looked at me. I shrugged.

"Okay. Let's go," Alex said as he started to walk up the hill.

Jon touched my stomach as he walked by.

"All aboard the exploration station!" Tierrah said as she pulled on an imaginary train horn cord. "Let's go down to the dock and check out the boats."

"Sounds sketchy. Let's go," I agreed.

The boys went one way and we went another.

We got down to the docks and watched some kids feed what looked like a hundred fish all coming up for food. We passed a few boats and came up to a boat that had a couple of guys who looked our age. They both stared at us as we walked by. They looked gruffy and had rough looking beards and worn out clothes.

"They probably don't see many brown people around here," I joked.

"Or just two hotties in swimsuits, Jasmine."

"Whatever you say."

Their boat was the second to last on the dock. We looked out over the lake for a minute and then turned to go back. One of the guys approached us.

"You girls aren't from around here," he said taking his hat off.

"What makes you think that?" Tierrah asked without skipping a beat.

"Well. This here area is always the same people. Same people. Same boats. Same everything. Right, Sven?" He turned around and looked at the other guy.

"It's Memorial Day weekend, Garrett. I've seen people all day that we don't know."

"All familiar faces though," Garrett replied with his hand in the air. "These faces have never been here."

I looked at Tierrah. Her eyes were wide.

"This your boat?" she asked. "Or your parents? Or what?"

"This is my boat," Sven answered.

"Can we have a ride?" Tierrah asked.

I'd say I couldn't believe she asked two total strangers for a ride on their boat, but then

I'd be lying. If she wouldn't had asked right then, I would have.

"You want to come out on the lake with us?" Sven looked shocked.

"Is that okay?" I asked. "We aren't killers, but if you're scared then that's okay."

They both laughed.

"Hop aboard," Sven said. "Garrett, get the rope."

Tierrah and I climbed onto the boat. Garrett handed us each a drink. Sven started the boat and pulled away from the dock. I was excited. A little scared. A lot nervous. But very excited.

"Can I play some jams?" Tierrah asked as she pulled out her phone.

"Yes, please." Garrett answered.

She started a playlist and we laughed and enjoyed our drinks and danced around a bit.

We learned that Garrett and Sven had been friends their entire lives and grew up on the lake. We were the first non-family members that they had ever taken on a ride. They were both twenty-six and loved eating fish.

We were out on the water for a little over an hour. The sun started going down.

"Jon is going to trip," I said when we got close to the dock.

"If he trips out then he is crazy, Jasmine. Jon isn't going to trip out. They went and did their thing and we did ours." Tierrah laughed. "You two are dumb."

We exchanged numbers with Garrett and Sven and thanked them for the ride. We hopped off the boat and headed back to our spot.

Alex and Jon were sitting next to a fire they had made.

"Where were you guys?" Alex asked looking at Jon though instead of us.

Jon didn't say a word or even look up at us. Tierrah filled them in on our adventure.

"You two are too trustworthy," Alex said to her after she finished her story.

Jon wore a fake smile. It looked fake anyways.

"You guys get any service?" I finally chimed in.

"No service. So, no one else is coming," Jon answered.

"That's too bad." I said as I grabbed a drink and Lunchable from the cooler.

"It is too bad," Jon said, looking at me but still not smiling.

Alex looked at me. "Yeah, so Nate isn't going to be able to come." He looked back at Jon.

Tierrah stood there with her hands on her hips. "You two are being awkward as hell." She laughed. "Toss me a Lunchable."

We sat at the fire and ate and drank and laughed and joked and played music. After a couple of hours I got extremely tired.

"I think I'm going to go to sleep so I have energy for tomorrow," I said.

I stood up and attempted to add some sticks to the fire.

"Seriously?" Jon asked.

"What's up? I'm so tired. Maybe you will get lucky and get some phone service."

"Come on," he said putting his hands in the air as he stood up.

"Let her go." Tierrah laughed. "I need her to be awake tomorrow."

"I've got to close my eyes or I'm not going to make it," I said yawning.

"Go then." Alex laughed. "What are you waiting for?"

"Yeah, what are you waiting for?" Jon said as he sat back down.

"Okay. Well. Goodnight." I turned and headed to our tent.

I climbed inside and immediately closed my eyes. A couple of hours later I woke up to Jon whispering my name.

"What do you want?" I could barely open my eyes.

"Come join us. We have more food and I miss you. I'm sorry about earlier. I just can't believe you went with those guys."

"I went with those guys while you went looking for service to have another girl join us."

"Jasmine, I went to try and get a hold of Nate."

"And that girl!"

"She's not here. So what is your problem?"

"She would be here if you had service."

"Only because you told me to invite her! Stop this shit. You're being a bitch."

"Really, Jon?"'

He had never called me a name before. Especially not a bitch.

"I'm sorry," he said as he tried to kiss me.

I pushed him away.

"You know what?" I sat up. "I'm sorry too, okay?"

"Jasmine, stop."

"Really. Everything is fine. I'm sorry. I'm going back to sleep. I'll see you in the morning."

"Okay, Jasmine. I know you're mad. But okay. I'll leave you alone."

"Goodnight, Jon," I said as he stared at me.

I could see the hurt in his eyes. I knew he could see it in mine, too.

"I love you, Jasmine."

"Yep. Love you, too."

He crawled out of the tent and zipped it closed. I laid back down and immediately fell back asleep.

27

I woke up the next morning and it took me a second to recollect where I was and why I felt so cold. Tierrah was hedge hogged in the corner of the tent. Our tent was unzipped. *Well there's a murder waiting to happen.*

I slowly opened the tent's crawl space and peeked out as if I was scared of what I might see. I kind of was. I squinted as my eyes met the sun. I looked over at the guy's tent. Jon's head was poking out, but he wasn't smiling. He stared me. He crawled out quickly and stumbled over a tree root towards me with his arms reaching in my direction. I caught him by his hand. I took his other hand and joined him in the cold.

"Brrrrr," I exaggerated.

"You want me to hold you?"

"Yes. But I'm okay. I'm sorry for being a bitch last night."

"I'm sorry I called you that, Jasmine. You're perfect. I was being selfish."

"I was being jealous."

"Let's go down to the water." He put his hand around my waist.

We walked in silence. I could tell he was nervous. His arm and hand felt so warm. I wrapped mine around him as well and took in his warmth. He squeezed me.

"So. You're not mad?" He lifted my chin with his hand.

"No, Jon." I gave his cheek a kiss.

"Good. Because I love you. And respect you."

"I know, Jon."

I looked back to the campsite and saw Alex stretching outside of the guy's tent.

"We had a wild time after you fell asleep," Jon said, putting his hands on his head and bending his back backwards.

"Oh?"

"Yeah. I tried to wake you but."

"Yeah, I remember that part."

"I'm sorry, Jasmine."

"Stop. Let's go. I'm starving."

Tierrah woke up and was crawling out of the tent by the time we made it back up the hill.

"Good morning, beauties!" Alex said, still stretching. "Let's go get some grub!"

"Let's do our tents first," Tierrah suggested. "That way we can get going and meet with Ken."

We worked in silence as we packed up and broke the tents down. I made eye contact with Jon a couple of times. He smiled each time. I didn't smile back. I was silently still throwing a fit about being called a bitch. I wasn't mad, just still in shock. And he knew it.

"I'm starving. Maybe we should have gotten food first," Tierrah said as I closed her full trunk. "Let's go eat."

Jon grabbed my hand. Alex led us to the café.

"Mmmm. Fresh fish in the morning." Jon sniffed loudly and buried his nose in my neck.

"I'll push you in, Jon." I grabbed him by the arm.

"I've got five on it!" Alex laughed.

The café was empty. We sat outside on the deck. The waitress took Alex and Tierrah's order and then looked at me.

"She'll take two eggs over medium and a side of bacon with extra bacon and toast," Jon said smiling.

"Seriously, Jon?" Tierrah laughed. "Is he right?" She looked at me.

"Yes, ma'am. Thank you."

Jon ordering for me was nothing new.

I checked my phone as Jon began to order for himself. Still no service.

"I've got two bars," Tierrah said as I held my phone up in the air.

"Me too. This is why you need iPhone, Jas," Alex said.

I put my phone away and watched as Jon filled his coffee with sugar.

"You're going to be sick." I sighed.

He looked at me smiling as he continued to pour. Our food came quick and we all ate everything on our plate, famished from the night before.

"Carry me." I rested my head on Jon's shoulder.

Tierrah rolled her eyes.

We paid our tabs and headed back to Tierrah's car. The guys walked ahead of us.

"Ken is going to swoop me and then we will come get you and then go get them," she said while typing on her phone. "Is something going on with you two?"

"What do you mean?" I asked, trying to look clueless.

"Well, last night he said he went and tried waking you up and you got mad. Like. Real mad."

"Oh?"

"Yeah. I told him to stop being a little bitch."

"Tierrah."

"What? He was. And it worked. He stopped."

"I'm fine. We're fine. He was just being a douche."

We got to the car and rode back to town in silence. Jon dozed off on Alex's shoulder. When I finally got service I had twenty-something texts. Twenty were from my mom. I only replied to one.

"I'm alive, mother. No service. Headed back."

I got lost in the clouds daydreaming about how the night before would have gone if I weren't such a prude or if that girl would have come. I wondered who all would be at the river. I thought about JJ.

28

I woke up to Jon tapping on the window. I had fallen asleep on the drive home as well. We were out front of Jon's apartment. He turned around before I could roll the window down and began to head up his stairs. Tierrah started to pull out.

"Don't they need their stuff?" I asked straightening up.

"They already unloaded." Tierrah laughed. "You were sleeping hard. And loud. Your phone has been going off like crazy, too."

I looked down at my phone. My mother was upset that my explanation wasn't good enough earlier.

"I'm going to drop you and then run and get Ken. Give me thirty. Be ready."

"Okay," I answered.

"Just leave your stuff in the trunk. We will sort it out later."

We pulled up to my apartment. I stretched as I got out of the car. Tierrah pulled off. I was surprised how well rested I felt. I climbed my stairs and went inside.

I called for Madalynn. I had forgotten that my mother had her. Latika was happy to see me. She pranced from my room right up to me. I scooped her in my arms and held her body to my face.

"Shower time?"

I sat her down and walked straight to the shower. She followed. I undressed and was in and out within five minutes. My phone went off again.

Momma: ANSWER ME JASMINE NICOLE
Me: It's Jasmine NICOEL mother
Momma: Okay smartass. Come and get your daughter
Me: I said tonight mom. We are going to the river
Momma: I'm going to charge you for this
Me: Okay mom
Momma: I'm just going to keep her. She is happy here and you don't care enough to check on her or let us know you are safe
Me: Mom we had zero service. I'm sorry. We are home now and about to head to the river
Momma: Drive safe. Where's Jon?
Me: We will. He is home. Kiss Madalynn for me
Momma: I love you

Me: Love you too

    I grabbed my suit and put it back on. I thought about grabbing a different one, but Jon liked that one the best because it somewhat matched his swim trunks.

    I cleaned Latika's litterbox, chugged a water, and locked up to head downstairs. Ken and Tierrah pulled up right as I was throwing Latika's poop into the dumpster. Ken rolled her window down and turned the music up.

    "You miss me?" she yelled out of the window.

    I smiled as I got in the back seat.

    "I can't believe you're actually ready," Tierrah said as I buckled up. "Let's hope the guys are, too."

    I called Jon on the way over. He said they were ready and would be right down.

    "I'm glad you ladies had a good time." Ken said looking back at me as she parked. "Tierrah told me about Sven and Garrett. You guys are lucky you didn't get kidnapped." She laughed.

    "I thought the same thing! I was nervous, but hey, we got to ride on a boat."

"You two are ridiculous," Tierrah chimed in. "Jasmine and I could have easily kicked their asses."

I looked out the window and saw Jon and Alex coming down the stairs. Jon kept eye contact with me the entire time smiling. Well. I tell myself he was making eye contact with me. He had on his huge opaque black sunglasses. He also had on his hat that I loved. His hair looked perfect beneath it. Jon got in on the other side and slid to the middle as Alex put his cooler into the trunk.

"You smell so good," he said as he kissed my shoulder. His lips were red and cold from eating a popsicle.

"You too." I smiled. "You excited? I'm excited to bring you. We will have to get in the mud pit."

"I'm not getting in the mud pit, but yes, I'm excited."

Alex joined us in the car.

"You guy's ready?" Ken looked at us through the rear view mirror.

"Let's do it!" Alex answered.

We blared a CD I had just made for Tierrah on the way. Every other vehicle we passed on the highway was hauling a boat or canoes. I gazed out the window. I daydreamed about how the river would be and about how wonderful life had been lately. I thought about making it official with Jon.

Why do you keep passing up perfection? Life would be so good. I knew I could spend forever with him. *There's no way JJ would give you forever.* I looked at Jon. The wind was blowing his hair perfectly. He grabbed my hand, smiled, and squeezed.

29

I showed Ken where to turn to go down to the party side of the river. We pulled in slowly behind two cars. The owner of the land was stopping and looking in the cars as they pulled in. *Surely he won't remember me.* It had been a year. We pulled up. Tierrah rolled down her window.

"Hello, ladies," he said with a smile. "Nope! Not her." He immediately pointed at me. "Turn the vehicle around."

"Come on," Tierrah begged.

"Turn your vehicle around, please. You're welcome on the other side. Not here."

We pulled forward and turned around in the lot.

"Sorry, guys," I laughed. "I'm banned!"

We drove to the other side of the river and found a spot to park. We filled Jon's cooler, took off our excess clothing so we only had on our swimsuits, and waded through the river to the forbidden side.

"You're so bad." Jon said when we made it to the party side.

"You're guilty now too, you know? We all are," Tierrah said, sitting down on the cooler. "Guilty by association!"

"Not me," Ken said while tightening her shoelaces. "Ya'll are on your own with this one."

"Jasmine! Tierrah! Hey!" Gio's voice filled the air over the hundred other voices and music coming from numerous cars.

"Yes! We just got here." I hugged her and picked her up. "Where are you parked?"

"Girl, it's wild here!" She put her hands on her hips. "Hey Jonnnn." She smiled at Jon.

"Hello, Gio." He smiled.

Alex picked up the cooler and we headed down the dirt road. I knew just about everyone. This was apparently the place to be this year. My name was being called in every which direction. We stopped every few minutes to talk to someone. I introduced Jon to everyone. He was so happy and all smiles.

"Everyone is so friendly!" He smiled as he put his hand on my shoulder.

We swam for a bit in the river until my friend Joni called my name from the shore.

"Joni!" I went to join her. "I'm so happy you're here!"

"Right, Bug? This place is packed. And no fights. I'm loving it."

"Where are you going now?"

"I'm headed to the swing. I don't think I can do it, but this guy thinks I can." She nodded her head to the long curly haired guy who was approaching us. His hair was slicked back and dripping wet.

"Let's go, chicken." He picked her up and spun her around.

"Come with us," she said as Jon joined me.

"This is Jon." I grabbed Jon's hand.

Joni looked at our interlocked hands.

"Oh? Okay. Let's go, Jon!"

Jon smiled. We followed them to the rope swing.

"No way am I going on that. Jon?" I watched as someone swung and did a flip into the water.

"You going to go, Joni?" He looked at Joni.

"Nope!"

"She's too scared," the guy said to Jon.

"Show me how it's done!" Joni softly pushed Jon.

He didn't answer. He looked at me and then climbed to the top of the crane, grabbed the rope, and jumped.

When he let go of the rope he yelled, "You're next, Joni!"

Joni laughed. "He's a keeper, Bug. I like him. And he likes you."

"I think so, too," I agreed.

Jon joined us back on the shore. Tierrah, Ken, and Alex came walking up.

"What's next?" Alex asked as he rung out his shorts.

I shrugged and we walked down to the end of the road. Nothing was going on so we walked back to the water. I showed them the mud pit that was filled with people. None of us wanted to get in.

"There's a cliff back there that people are jumping off of," Alex said, pointing past the pit.

"Well, let's go!" Ken said grabbing my hand. "Don't let me fall. These shoes are awful."

We walked until we got to a cliff that had a pond-looking area below it. People were lined up and jumping off.

"No way," I immediately said. "There's just no way."

"It's not that high, babe." Jon laughed.

"Yeah, babe!" I didn't even realize Gio was standing next to me.

"Oh hey girl, hey. I didn't even see you down there."

"Funny, Jasmine," she said, using her hand to block the sun as she looked up at me.

"I'm going," Jon said. He handed me his hat and glasses. "I think our cooler is with Joni."

"Okay, hurry," I said as I put his glasses on top of my head.

He gave me an awkward hug and followed some guys that were headed to the top of the cliff.

"You going to jump?" I asked Alex.

"Hell no. No telling what is in that water."

We waited a few minutes before we saw Jon. Three guys jumped before him. The last one did a flip. Tierrah cheered and everyone clapped.

Then Jon appeared. We all started to yell. He had a big smile. He called something down to me but I couldn't hear. Then he jumped.

I was surprised with how big of a splash his skinny body made. He came up laughing as he flipped his hair back. He swam over and wiped his eyes on my shoulder. I was relieved to see my necklace hadn't come off.

"The water is warm," he said as I handed him his glasses. "You know what that means?"

"You're gross," I said, putting his hat on his head. "Don't lose my necklace, please."

"I was going to jump again."

"No. Let's get back to the river. I want to swim some more and not in this hole."

"Go again, Jon," Tierrah said, winking.

"I'm getting a better view," Alex said as he turned to walk around to the other side.

I crossed my arms to pout.

"Babe." He put his hat on my head. "One more time and you're in charge."

I don't know why I decided to continue to pout. He was having a great time. We all were. Maybe I wanted the attention. Either way, he knew I was pouting.

"I'll be right back. We will swim and then find someone grilling, okay?"

I took his glasses and put them on.

He turned around to go. He stopped walking and came back to me.

"Kiss?" he asked, smiling.

"Jon, just go," I smiled.

"Come on, Jasmine. Just once so everyone can see me kissing the prettiest girl here."

"You're crazy," I said, shaking my head no. "No. Just go. Hurry."

He turned to walk off. He stopped again and turned to face me. He blew me a kiss and tossed me my necklace. I caught his kiss and put it to my cheek. I had missed the necklace, so I picked it up and put it around my neck. He laughed.

"I love you, Jasmine."

"Love you. Go."

I looked around and found Alex across the water. Ken, Gio, Tierrah, and I waited until we saw Jon again. Again, there were two other jumpers before him. The place was starting to fill up with eager jumpers.

Jon came to the edge. He was scoping out the hole. I saw him squinting as he looked in our direction. He waved. We all cheered his name.

As he jumped I called out his name three times. When he hit the water I entered the hole to meet him with a kiss by the shore when he came up.

The ripples in the water disappeared. The water was still. I looked over at Alex. As he stared back, all the sounds of the outside disappeared. *Come on, Jon. This shit isn't funny.*

I took a step forward. Jon's arm came up. Only his arm. It was splashing around. I started to walk towards him.

"Jon! Come on!"

He went back under.

"Jon!" I screamed and looked at Alex.

"Alex! His head didn't come up!"

I dove into the dark water and started to feel around before I had to come back up for air.

"Jon!"

I went back under and opened my eyes. I couldn't see anything through the muddy water. I tried to scream his name under the water but started to choke and had to come back up for air again. When I came up there were people all around the edge of the hole.

"Help me! Somebody help me! Somebody help him! Get in! Fucking get in!"

A few guys jumped in. I went back under. I came back up. I went back under. I came back up. I went back under. *You were a lifeguard for six years, Jasmine. You will save him. This is it. Save him. He's fine. Look again. He's fine.* I came back up.

"Where is he?" I screamed. "Alex!"

Gio pulled me from the water. People started to surround me. I couldn't breathe. I could barely make out anyone's faces through my tears.

"Back up! Back the fuck up!" I heard Tierrah yell as she was getting people to back away from me.

"Tierrah." I looked at her.

"Ken called 911. They're coming." She said with tears in her eyes.

I walked back to the shore and sat down. There were still two guys searching for him. They searched for twenty minutes straight. They'd come up and then they'd go back under. I had never seen them before in my life. One of the guys approached me.

"I'm sorry. I can't anymore. Did someone call 911?"

I stared at him. I couldn't speak.

"Someone called, yes. Thank you." Tierrah spoke for me.

"Thank you," I managed to say.

Forty-five minutes later the ambulance arrived. They slowly put on their scuba gear. I watched their every move. I wanted to scream and tell them to go faster. I saw one of them laugh to another.

"They're fucking laughing! They are FUCKING laughing!" My voice was cracked.

"Baby girl. They're getting in. They will find him." Gio squeezed my hand.

"He will make it. Right?" I asked knowing the answer.

"We will see. I don't know, baby. I don't know."

"We need to get out of here and go to the hospital." Ken put her hand on my arm.

"I'm not leaving until I see him." I pulled away.

"They are bringing him to where my mother is. I just got off of the phone with her."

"I'm not moving until I see him."

Another forty-five minutes passed. The hole was surrounded by people. No one was smiling. Most of them were crying. I felt like everyone I had ever had as a friend was there. Not only that, but as each came to hug me all I could think about was the exact moment just a couple hours before that I was introducing them to Jon and having him shake their hand.

"Got him!" A diver said as he came up. "Get the board!"

I was confused. If he got him then why wasn't Jon out of the water?

Gio grabbed my hand as they put the board in the water. I looked at Alex. We stared at each other before looking back to the water. The men put the board under and came back up a moment later with Jon. He wasn't moving. He looked pale.

"Jon!" I screamed. "Jon!"

"We have to go now," Kendra said pulling my arm to follow her this time. "I will get us there. We have to go now. I already went and got my car."

All sound disappeared again. I kept looking back as she and now Tierrah pulled me towards the car.

Jon.

31

As we pulled away I realized that everyone from the river had walked down to the hole to see what had happened. The crowd of people opened so that we could get through. As we drove through the entrance the owner made eye contact with me and stared the entire time as we passed.

I held Jon's glasses and hat tight and removed my bottle opener from his key chain. I tugged on the wooden beaded necklace around my neck.

I had Alex call Nate as I got Jon's mother's number from a friend.

"What's wrong?" Kells asked after she repeated the number to me.

"I can't say right now, Kells. I'll call you back."

I dialed Jon's mother's number. She answered.

"Yes?"

"It's me. Jasmine."

"Everything okay, Jasmine? What's wrong?"

"No. I'm sorry. It's Jon. He. He's."

"Jon? What's wrong? Tell me what's wrong!" I heard the panic in her voice.

"He jumped and he didn't come back up. He didn't come back up from the water."

"What?" she screamed into the phone. "Where are you? Where is Jon? Jon? Where is Jon? Jasmine, I need you to tell me!"

"I'm sorry. He didn't come back up. He drowned. Jon drowned. They have him in the ambulance now. I'm so sorry."

"Where is he, Jasmine?"

"I don't know where we are going. Just get up and dressed and head to Joplin. I will call you right back. I'm sorry. I don't know."

"Okay." She hung up the phone.

Ken sped us to the hospital. Her mother worked where Jon would be taken so we were able to pull into the back. We started to walk to the doors and my legs went out on me. I sat on the curb. Everyone else went inside. Ken's mother came and sat next to me. She put her arms around me.

"Is he going to be okay?" I asked her as I put my face between my knees.

"I'm very sorry, Jasmine. He was under for too long. He didn't make it. He has been gone for a while now."

I cried. She held me. I handed her my phone.

"Please call his mother."

"Does she know?"

"Yes. But not everything. She is on her way. Please explain it to her for me."

As she called Jon's mother I began talking to God.

Why? Why Jon? Why this? Why now? How could you? He wasn't ready. He belongs here. Please. Wake me up, God. Please let me wake up. Please.

Ken's mother hung up the phone and held her hand out to me to help me up. I slowly stood and wiped my eyes.

"You will get through this, Jasmine." She squeezed my hand.

We entered the hospital together. We went to room where Jon's mother was. She was pale white. I held her while she cried. I handed her his hat and keys.

I don't remember much more of what happened at the hospital. I don't even remember how I got home. I don't remember what happened next with Tierrah, Ken, or even Alex. I vaguely remember calling my mother. She cried on the other end of the phone. However, I'll never forget that first night.

I got to my apartment and went to let Madalynn out. I had forgotten she was with my mother. I stared at myself in the mirror. My eyes were swollen. I got a washcloth and washed my face. I was awake. I was still hoping to wake up.

I heard my phone go off in the living room. I grabbed it and put it on silent without looking at it. I had over fifty text messages and twenty something missed calls. I sat my phone down and went to my room.

And then I saw it. Jon's sock. *What?* I picked it up and examined it. I cried. I came to the conclusion it wasn't the missing sock. *Don't be crazy.* I opened my sock drawer to toss it in. I pulled the drawer open and there was the match. My stomach dropped.

"Jon?" I called out. "Jon if you're here, I'm sorry. I'm so sorry, Jon. I love you and I'm sorry."

I looked in the mirror. *Stop it, Jasmine.*

I put the socks on and got in bed. I prayed and asked God to allow me to see him in my dreams. I cried myself to sleep.

I didn't dream of Jon.

The next few days seemed to run into each other. I didn't work either jobs. My friends and family were reaching out to me for support. I barely kept in contact with Alex.

Jon's mother and I spoke only on the phone. Jon was her only child. She was lost and broken. She didn't understand and I couldn't fix it for her. My heart broke for her. It was hard not feeling responsible for his death. I was the one who brought him. I was the one who didn't save him. And each time I spoke to his mother I found myself apologizing for his death. Each time I felt more and more responsible.

The day came for his funeral. I had spent the previous nights writing a poem to read to everyone. I read it what seemed like a thousand times that morning.

When it was time to get ready to go I panicked when I couldn't find the black undershirt I wanted to wear. I sat down on my bed and cried. After I caught my breath I stood up and the undershirt was on top of my laundry pile. I felt sick.

"Jon?" I called out. "Jon, please. Please come to me in my dreams. Please be with me today and always. Please, Jon."

Stop it, Jasmine.

I finished getting ready.

When I arrived at the funeral I wasn't surprised to see so many people. I sat through the service until it was my time to speak. I walked to the front and to the podium. I stood for a second as I looked over at Jon's body.

Breathe, Jasmine.

I began to read.

I was with you every day and nearly every night,
Inseparable the last few months, even when we'd fight.
I remember the talks, every one that we had,
Some were good and some left us sad.
But through it all, no matter what we were told,
One thing we had were each other's hands to hold.
We talked about Lily and how you had missed her,
Y'all were amped to go to Florida, you loved your little sister.

When we talked about Nathon you never called him friend,
You only referred to him as brother right to the very end.
You told me about your mom and how she was the coolest I'd ever meet,
I believe she knows how much you loved her, we're trying to keep her on her feet.
Alex had five on it, you claimed to have ten,
We always had something to laugh about when it was just me you and him.
I hate that you won't be with me the first time I meet your dad,
It's time to change the subject now, these words are making me sad.
For everyone who doesn't know, I gotta tell them so here I go.
His last breakfast was at the lake, he couldn't wait to go to the river that day,
He had ice-cream for lunch with Alex, his lips were so red,
He was going to drive his car, but rode with us instead.
We got to the river and he wore the biggest smile,
He met so many people and we were only there a little while.

He jumped off the rope swing to help my friend out,
Let's go to the cliff now everyone started to shout.
He said Jasmine I'm having a blast I'm so happy we came,
I'm glad we're besties. I told him the same.
He jumped off the cliff twice, the story goes from there,
Just know that he went happy, that's something I wanted to share.
So now we're letting you go, my dear Jon,
But in our hearts, we'll forever hold on.
Losing you was like losing a lung,
But you told me once you wanted to stay forever young.
I love you, Jon.

    I immediately stepped down from the podium after I was finished. His mother hugged me and cried on my shoulder for a second before she returned to the stand and allowed others to come speak.

    When the time came, I went and looked at Jon. He looked great. I placed my wooden necklace in his hands. I rested my hands on top of his and looked at his face.

"I love you, Jon. I'm yours."

After everyone had finished we drove to the gravesite where his body would be buried. After his service was complete I touched his coffin one last time to say goodbye. Tierrah and Brooke too me to dinner afterwards.

33

I spent the next few days spending time with Alex and whoever stopped by. I stayed home mostly. I returned to the preschool and was met with support from my boss and co-workers. I wasn't ready to return to Savannah's yet.

Jon's sister, cousins, and Nate all got koi tattoos similar to Jon's that covered the upper half of their arms. I got his initials tattooed on my right wrist where I knew I could see and be reminded about him every day for the rest of my life. Alex got his initials on his arm.

My first day back to Savannah's was hard. Vince said it was ridiculous that I got a tattoo of someone I had just met. I flipped him off. He apologized.

I overheard my last table for the evening talking about the boy who had drowned that used to work there. As I got closer to their table they asked me if I knew him.

"He was my boyfriend. My best friend." I walked off crying and didn't return.

They left me a fifty dollar tip. I quit two days later.

JJ got out of prison the next month. He was upset about the tattoo, but never said too much about Jon.

Jon's sister adopted Latika.

Alex and I eventually stopped hanging out.

I found myself hoping to get another sign that Jon was with me. Nothing had happened since the sock or the undershirt. I cried most nights and almost every day driving to and from the preschool as I blared the CD we always listened to.

Then it happened. What I had been praying and hoping and waiting for.

I opened my eyes and there he was. I was laughing that he had put his shirt on backwards. He laughed as he turned it around and stared at me. I asked him what was wrong, but he didn't reply. He just stared at me. The wind blew his hair and he looked away. Then it hit me.

"Jon!" My voice was muffled.

He smiled.

"Jon, don't let me wake up!" My voice cracked as tears started to pour from my eyes.

He walked towards me and put my face in his hands. He kissed my cheek and leaned in to whisper in my ear.

"See you."

The End

The years have gone by way too fast
With only memories of your face that will always last
It feels just like yesterday we woke up at the lake
Then a few hours later I made phone call that I never imagined I'd have to make
I remember your smile that you had that day
I remember trying to hide my love for you in every single way
I remember the last thing you said to me before you took that dive
I remember the way you made me feel when you were still alive
I'm sorry we couldn't find you I hope you know we tried
I swear I felt you with me that first night as I cried
And now it's years later and I still can't believe you're gone
So every day I look at my wrist and it keeps me going on

I want to say I wish I could go back
But then I wouldn't have had the twins
If we had the gift to turn back time
Then who would really win?
Too often I cry about that day
Then Jmar says Momma so I wipe them away
But if only just once I could hear you say
Shut up, Jasmine it will all be okay
But I can't so I push all my thoughts away
And live my life of work and play
And next thing I know May is here again
So I count out my what ifs of who where and when
And I count down the days before I'm standing at your grave
Taking a flower that I'll always save
Rubbing your initials printed on my wrist
Wondering what it'd be if it wasn't like this

Made in the USA
Lexington, KY
05 March 2018